All About the Kingdom

*Cycle A Sermons for
Proper 24 Through Thanksgiving
Based on the Gospel Texts*

David G. Rogne

CSS Publishing Company, Inc.
Lima, Ohio

ALL ABOUT THE KINGDOM

FIRST EDITION
Copyright © 2013
by CSS Publishing Co., Inc.

Published by CSS Publishing Company, Inc., Lima, Ohio 45807. All rights reserved. No part of this publication may be reproduced in any manner whatsoever without the prior permission of the publisher, except in the case of brief quotations embodied in critical articles and reviews. Inquiries should be addressed to: CSS Publishing Company, Inc., Permissions Department, 5450 N. Dixie Highway, Lima, Ohio 45807.

Scripture quotations are from the New Revised Standard Version of the Bible. Copyright 1989 by the Division of Christian Education of the National Council of the Churches of Christ in the USA. Used by permission.

Library of Congress Cataloging-in-Publication Data

Rogne, David George, 1934-
 All About the Kingdom : Cycle A Sermons for Proper 24 Through Thanksgiving Based on the Gospel Texts / David G. Rogne. -- FIRST EDITION.
     pages cm
   ISBN 0-7880-2710-7 (alk. paper)
 1. Bible. N.T. Gospels--Sermons. 2. Sermons, American--21st century. 3. Pentecost season--Sermons. 4. Church year sermons. 5. Common lectionary (1992). Year A. I. Title.

BS2555.54.R64 2013
252'.64--dc23

2012046837

For more information about CSS Publishing Company resources, visit our website at www.csspub.com, email us at csr@csspub.com, or call (800) 241-4056.

ISBN-13: 978-0-7880-2710-9
ISBN-10: 0-7880-2710-7   PRINTED IN USA

this is for Mary Jane,

a co-laborer in the kingdom

Table of Contents

Proper 24   7
Pentecost 19
Ordinary Time 29
   Paying What's Due
   Matthew 22:15-22

Proper 25   15
Pentecost 20
Ordinary Time 30
   A Love Triangle
   Matthew 22:34-46

Reformation Day   23
   Being a True Disciple
   John 8:31-36

All Saints Day   33
   Hallelujah! Come On, Get Happy
   Matthew 5:1-12

Proper 26   43
Pentecost 21
Ordinary Time 31
   The Real Thing
   Matthew 23:1-12

Proper 27   51
Pentecost 22
Ordinary Time 32
   Always Ready
   Matthew 25:1-13

Proper 28   59
Pentecost 23
Ordinary Time 33
    Talented People
    Matthew 25:14-30

Christ the King Sunday   69
(Proper 29 / Pentecost 24 / Ordinary Time 34)
    Who Cares?
    Matthew 25:31-46

Thanksgiving Day   79
    Thanks-Giving Is Good for Everyone
    Luke 17:11-19

If You Like This Book...   87

Proper 24
Pentecost 19
Ordinary Time 29
Matthew 22:15-22

Paying What's Due

Then the Pharisees went and plotted to entrap him in what he said. So they sent their disciples to him, along with the Herodians, saying, "Teacher, we know that you are sincere, and teach the way of God in accordance with truth, and show deference to no one; for you do not regard people with partiality. Tell us, then, what you think. Is it lawful to pay taxes to the emperor, or not?" But Jesus, aware of their malice, said, "Why are you putting me to the test, you hypocrites? Show me the coin used for the tax." And they brought him a denarius. Then he said to them, "Whose head is this, and whose title?" They answered, "The emperor's." Then he said to them, "Give therefore to the emperor the things that are the emperor's, and to God the things that are God's." When they heard this, they were amazed; and they left him and went away.

In Joseph Heller's book *Catch-22*, an Air Force bombardier is desperately seeking relief from going out on the deadly missions he must fly each day. As he gets close to the number of missions that will allow him to be rotated, the number of missions needed for rotation keeps changing. He concludes that only a crazy person would keep flying those dangerous missions. He thinks he must be crazy, and therefore he should be sent home. His superiors agree with him that a crazy person should be sent home but only a sane person could recognize the danger involved. Therefore, anyone who sees the danger is not crazy. He is caught in catch-22.

On the day after people poured out of Jerusalem to greet Jesus and accompany him with palm branches and shouts of acclaim into the city, agents of two groups that had little use for each other, but even less use for Jesus, joined forces to keep Jesus from capitalizing on his warm welcome into the city. They intended to trap Jesus into taking a stand that would get him into trouble. Their means of entrapment was to be a catch-22 question: "Is it lawful to pay taxes to the emperor, or not?" If Jesus said "No," he could be accused of sedition and turned over to the Romans. If he said "Yes," he would at once lose the sympathy of many of his supporters, who naturally hated the Roman tax and expected that if Jesus were the Messiah he would break the yoke of the Roman oppressors and not urge tribute to them. Either way, the religious leaders would achieve their end.

Jesus asked for a coin, a denarius, the coin used to pay the head tax to Rome. He asked the agents to verify whose image was on it. "The emperor's," they said. "Very well," said Jesus, "give therefore to the emperor the things that are the emperor's, and to God the things that are God's" (v. 21). With that answer Jesus put responsibility for one's conduct back on the individual. Each one would decide how to respond. Those words still have a message for us.

The first thing Jesus does is acknowledge that there are some things the citizens owe to their government. One of those things is obedience to its just laws. Obeying the law sometimes means we have to abide by restrictions on our actions for the sake of the common good. I read recently about a dairyman who objected to having his cows inspected for tuberculosis. He ran the inspector off with a shotgun. In justification of his drastic action he said, "I am free, white and 21, and no government official is going to tell me how to run my business." What he forgot is that his freedom to sell milk ends where the rights of babies to have healthful food begin. Because most of us see things only from our own point of view there are laws protecting the general welfare, and good citizens need to respect those laws, even when it is personally distasteful.

Another thing a country may expect when its government is responsive to the needs of its citizens is loyalty. Stonewall Jackson, the Confederate general, was marching in Virginia in 1863. Long columns of soldiers were strung out. The general rode back, watching the men, and saw one limping. He called out, "Do you think you'll make it, soldier?" The weary soldier responded, "I guess I'll make it, but I hope to God I never have to show my loyalty to another country." Loyalty can often require us to make great sacrifices.

Even those who break the law may have a sense of the importance of loyalty. Some years ago, an indignant thief called the New York office of the FBI to confess that he stole a suitcase in Grand Central Station. "It's full of blueprints and other stuff that looks like secret military information," he said. "I think the guy I stole it from is a spy. I've checked it in one of the public lockers and I'm mailing you the key. I may be a thief, but I'm a loyal American thief." The country that has nurtured us can reasonably call for our loyalty.

Still another thing a government such as ours ought to be able to expect of its citizens is responsible involvement in making things better. When heavyweight boxing champion Joe Louis was asked why, in view of American discrimination against blacks, he was happy to serve in the United States Army during World War II he responded, "Man, whatever is wrong with my country ain't nothin' Hitler can fix!" In our country, commitment to active citizenship is important. The contributions of morally conscientious Christian citizens are particularly needed.

A government also has a right to expect that its citizens will pay for the benefits they receive. For the Jews of Jesus' day, the head tax was particularly repugnant because it was paid to a foreign power. The most conservative Jews thought of themselves as a nation ruled only by God. Therefore, to pay the tax was to acknowledge the existence of another king. But Jesus points out that there are indeed earthly rulers, and it is appropriate to pay for the services they provide. We benefit from public services: law and order, fire protection, water, education, defense, the justice system, and social security. That means we have obligations to our country, state, and community. It was pointed out during the debates over taxation that thousands of persons whose annual income exceeded $200,000 a year were able to avoid any payment of taxes. That constitutes taking something and not paying for it. One of the things that stirred up public sentiment against the hotel owner Leona Helmsley a number of years ago was her alleged statement: "Only little people pay taxes." Her feeling was that the better off one is, the less necessity there is to pay for what one receives. This is a long way from Jesus' admonition to give to the emperor the things that are the emperor's.

One further thing the citizens of a republic owe to the government is continuous scrutiny of its policies. One commentator on the American scene urges us to behave toward our country as women behave toward the men they love. A loving wife will do anything for her husband, except to stop criticizing and trying to improve him. We should cast the same affectionate, but sharp, glance at our country. We should love it but insist on telling it all its faults.

It is not the critic who is a danger to a republic, but the noisy chauvinist. For many years a leading newspaper in this country had on its editorial masthead: "My country, right or wrong." Many patriotic Americans accepted that as their philosophy too and felt called to defend whatever policy the government might have on a particular issue. They may have done better to accept the whole statement as Carl Schurz stated it in an address before Congress in 1872: "Our country, right or wrong. When right, to be kept right. When wrong, to be put right." "Pay to the emperor what is the Emperor's."

The second thing Jesus says is "(Give) to God the things that are God's" (v. 21). Surely one of the things due to God is worship. In the story on which the play *Fiddler on the Roof* is based, Tevya the dairyman prays three times a day. He addresses God, whom he loves, with affection, irony, sympathy, reverence, impudence, and hope. Every morning at sunrise he says his longing prayers with a prayer shawl over his head and other reminders of God on his brow and arm. When he comes to America, he is all the more determined to keep his relationship with God, for when people tell him that religion is superstition, he responds that if all the persecutions of the ages and all the bitterness of exploitation could not prevent him from repeating the prayers of his fathers, he certainly can't be made to fall away from them in the world of freedom. Worship gave Tevya his perspective.

In his book *How to Believe* (Garden City, New York: Doubleday & Company, 1953, p. 161), Ralph Sockman wrote:

> In our jobs we sit for five or six days a week like an Oriental weaver behind his loom busily fingering the threads of an intricate pattern. Every seventh day the Church, in her worship, calls us around in front of the loom to look at the pattern on which we have been working. She bids us compare the design of our days with the pattern shown us on Mount of Sinai and the Mount of the Beatitudes.

Worship is God's due, but those who do the worshiping are the beneficiaries.

Another thing we owe to God is service. "Just as you did it to one of the least of these who are members of my family, you did it to me," says Jesus (Matthew 25:40). Dr. Ernest Campbell, former minister of New York City's Riverside Church, tells how he became involved in social and political problems. He told of his experience in visiting a poor woman in nearby Harlem, who was grieving over the tragic death of her teenage son. He wanted to express Christian concern and bring the peace of God to this troubled woman. While he was praying with her, his prayer was interrupted by a rat scurrying out of a wastebasket and across the floor. The woman explained that all her efforts to get rid of rats were to no avail, because the whole building was infested and the superintendent refused to do anything about it. Dr. Campbell felt he needed to do something to help, so he spoke to the management, who would do nothing. When he checked with City Hall, he found that the authorities would do nothing either, unless he became actively involved in politics. So he became involved and something got done. What started out as a simple worship experience, a prayer, led to involvement and social action: service to "one of the least of these."

Still another thing that Christians owe to God is obedience. That obedience has often led to painful conflict. During the Nazi control of Germany, many groups had to decide to whom to be obedient. Helmuth von Moltke, leader of a persecuted Protestant group called the Kreisau Circle, was picked up by the Nazis for speaking out on behalf of conservative Christian principles. Eventually Moltke died for those principles. In his last letter to his wife before being executed, he wrote that he stood before Hitler's court not as a Protestant, not as a landowner, not as a noble, not as a Prussian, not even as a German. He stood before the court simply as a Christian and nothing else. The claims of God and the claims of Caesar are sometimes in conflict, and then we have to decide to whom we will be obedient.

One more thing that a Christian appropriately owes to God is loyalty. It would be nice if we always kept our loyalties separate and equal, like writing a check to the IRS to satisfy the state, and writing a check to the church to meet our responsibility to God. Unfortunately, it is not that simple. During World War II, a word was coined that speaks to the divided allegiances that confront all of us. The word is "traitriot" — a hybrid of the words "traitor" and "patriot." It pointed to the unhappy plight of those Japanese Americans who gave allegiance to the United States. For the time being at least, they had to turn their backs on Japan. From the time of Jesus' ministry, Christians have been aware that they are citizens of another homeland, and that dual citizenship sometimes requires painful choices.

The third thing I want to say is that when we are faced with painful choices, we must be careful that we do not look for the easiest way of resolving the problem. One of those seemingly easier ways is to allow others to make our tough decisions. Erich Fromm was a Jewish psychoanalyst living in Berlin when the Nazis came to power. Prior to that time he had assumed that humankind was coming of age. Instead, he witnessed with horror how the German people of the '30s gave up their freedom to Hitler as eagerly as their forefathers had fought for it. Out of his inquiry into how this could be so, came the realization that many people find that the freedom to choose is too much of a burden to bear. They would rather escape from freedom and rush to find some authority that would decide for them and allow them to be children again or even slaves. It is a constant temptation for all of us to abdicate moral responsibility and allow the government to decide for us what conduct is moral and what is not, or whether a certain war is morally justifiable or not. It is a temptation we must resist.

It is equally dangerous to turn governmental decisions over to the religious authorities. Jim Jones took his religious followers to Guyana to set up a new society with himself in charge. With no one to offer a contrary opinion, the leader became unbalanced and led his people to mass suicide. The church is no better at ruling the state than the state is at dictating morality.

Therefore, the decision as to what we render to Caesar

and what we render to God is never something that someone else can make for us if we are to be moral men and women. Not only must we pray for wisdom to make the choice, we must pray for the courage to act upon our choice. Thomas More was Lord Chancellor of England and a friend of King Henry VIII. But when Henry divorced his first wife and married Anne Boleyn, More disapproved and indicated that he could not vote to make these actions legitimate. More was arrested and charged with treason. In the play based on his life, *A Man for All Seasons*, More's daughter comes to him and urges him to break his oath in order to save his life, for the king has sworn to take More's life if he does not break the oath. More responds:

> When a man takes an oath, Meg, he's holding his own self in his own hands. Like water. And if he opens his fingers then, he needn't hope to find himself again... If we lived in a state where virtue was profitable, common sense would make us good, and greed would make us saintly. And we'd live like animals or angels in the happy land that needs no heroes. But since, in fact, we see that avarice, anger, envy, pride, sloth, lust, and stupidity commonly profit far beyond humility, chastity, fortitude, justice, and thought, and we have to choose (in order) to be human at all... why then we must stand fast a little — even at the risk of being heroes.
> (Robert Bolt, *A Man for All Seasons*)

"Give to the emperor the things that are the emperor's, and to God the things that are God's." But when they are in conflict, what is due to God comes first.

Proper 25
Pentecost 20
Ordinary Time 30
Matthew 22:34-46

A Love Triangle

When the Pharisees heard that he had silenced the Sadducees, they gathered together, and one of them, a lawyer, asked him a question to test him. "Teacher, which commandment in the law is the greatest?" He said to him, " 'You shall love the Lord your God with all your heart, and with all your soul, and with all your mind.' This is the greatest and first commandment. And a second is like it: 'You shall love your neighbor as yourself.' On these two commandments hang all the law and the prophets." Now while the Pharisees were gathered together, Jesus asked them this question: "What do you think of the Messiah? Whose son is he?" They said to him, "The son of David." He said to them, "How is it then that David by the Spirit calls him Lord, saying, 'The Lord said to my Lord, "Sit at my right hand, until I put your enemies under your feet" '? If David thus calls him Lord, how can he be his son?" No one was able to give him an answer, nor from that day did anyone dare to ask him any more questions.

Some people have a talent for getting to the core of things. Julius Caesar wrote a good-sized book titled *On the Gallic War.* It is still used as a textbook by students of Latin. However, Caesar was also able to cut through all the details and get to the nub of a matter. He wrote a sentence that has become a classic in condensation: *"Veni, Vidi, Vici"* — "I came, I saw, I conquered." That sums it all up.

In Jesus' day there was a group of people who pored over the ancient writings of Moses to look for every law in the book. They were called Pharisees and they were very scrupulous about the observance of all the religious laws. They counted up all the commandments of Moses and found that there were 613 of them; 248 of these were positive, and 365 of them were negative (one for every day of the year, they said). Instead of condensing and simplifying the commandments, they expanded and complicated them, so that what had started as a sincere desire to please God had become a terrible burden of ever-increasing requirements. They needed someone who could cut through all the burdensome requirements of the law and focus on its essence.

One of the Pharisees, perhaps dissatisfied with his own search for a meaningful religious life, approached Jesus and asked him which was the great commandment, the one that would satisfy God and oneself. In responding to the man, Jesus cut through all the liturgical requirements, taking from the book of Deuteronomy the requirement to love God, from Leviticus the requirement to love one's neighbor, and welding them together with an emphasis on love and not on the observance of a host of laws. For Jesus, meaningful religion was expressed in a triangle of love: love for God, love for others, and love for self. In that triangle of love is found the secret of a fulfilling life on earth and a foretaste of the life to come. Let's look more closely at what he said.

First, he said, we must love God. One of the ways we do this, he said, is with the heart. However, many of us who are sincere seekers after God are afraid to seek with the whole heart. We've met people who gave their hearts to Jesus, and the prospect frightens us. We want to keep cool, we want to keep our emotions in check, and we don't want to do something in the heat of emotion. As a consequence, we do such a good job of holding our hearts in check that we don't commit ourselves to anything, and we are poorer for it. I know a fellow who sincerely wants to get married. The only trouble is that he can't find the right girl. One is too young, another too old, one talks too much, another is too quiet, one has too much education, another not enough. The fellow goes around with a lot of girls, but he is unable to make a commitment to any. He is afraid to give his heart to anyone, and as a consequence he is never going to know the intimacy and fulfillment of a committed relationship.

A lot of people go around with God for a long time. They go to church, they go through the motions, they date God on Sunday, but there is no commitment. Consequently, there isn't much satisfaction in their religious life. They're afraid that if they get excited about God, it may cause them to get involved in some time-consuming issue; they may come to feel so strongly about something that they will have to act; they may feel obliged to take their stewardship seriously and begin to give a significant proportion of their income for the Lord's work; they may get sufficiently excited about what God is doing in their lives that they would have to share it with others. In short, loving God with our whole heart can be costly, but it is the only way to make the relationship rewarding. And it is rewarding in proportion to how much of ourselves we put into it.

Jesus also urges us to love God with our minds. There are some people who are content to separate faith and reason. For them faith is blind obedience to a certain interpretation or a certain person. But faith that is not balanced by reason can lead to destructive excesses. The followers of Jim Jones desired to move to Guyana and set up a new community for their betterment. They were a people of faith, seeking to do something worthwhile, but they forfeited their right to think for themselves. They were conditioned to think that faith left no room for doubt or questioning, and without any countervailing force to check his authority, their leader became a madman. When he told them to take poison and to give it to their children, more than 900 did so.

To love God does not require us to give up the capacity to think. God gave us our minds as well as our emotions, and if we are to be integrated individuals, mind and heart working together must lead us to a common goal. Sir James Jeans, the English astronomer and physicist, found that his studies of the universe led him more and more toward God. "We are discovering," he said, "that the universe gives evidence of being designed by a great mathematician." God is mind. Mind as well as heart beckons us to love God.

"And love God with all your soul," says Jesus. The soul is our most basic expression of who we are, and who we are is revealed by what we do. The proper response to the claims of God is not "true" or "false," but "yes" or "no." Instead of asking ourselves whether we believe or not, let us ask ourselves whether we have this day done one thing because God said "do it," or abstained from one thing because God said "do not do it." It is meaningless to say we believe in God if we don't do anything he tells us to do.

Do not expect that this call to love God is going to be satisfied by one big act of sacrifice. There are times in our lives when we might make some glorious sacrifice and go out in a blaze of glory, but rather than a blaze, most of us are confronted with many small campfires. We may think that giving our all to the Lord is like taking a $1,000 bill and laying it on the table saying, "Here's my life, Lord. Take it. I'm giving it to you." The reality is that the Lord sends us to the bank and has us cash the $1,000 bill for nickels and dimes. Then he asks us to go through life putting out a dime here, a nickel there. We would like to do it once and get it over with, but a life of loving God is spent a little at a time for as long as we live. This is loving God with all our soul.

Another side of this triangular relationship, Jesus says, is love of neighbor. One of the ways we diminish the force of these words is by restricting our understanding of who is our neighbor. When Albert Schweitzer went to Africa, he discovered a similar attitude among the natives. He found that to primitive people, the idea that one should be concerned for others had narrow limits. The native's concern is first to his blood relations and then to the members of his tribe, who represent to him the larger family. Schweitzer tells of asking ambulatory patients whom he had helped to give assistance to those who were confined to bed. But if the bedridden patient did not belong to the same tribe, the able-bodied patient would answer with wide-eyed innocence, "This man is not a brother of mine." Neither rewards nor threats could induce him to perform a service for a stranger.

Jesus calls us to a far more inclusive view of who is our neighbor. Charles Wolfe tells of being called out of a warm bed on a bitterly cold and icy night in Albany, New York. His brother was stranded downtown because his car wouldn't start. Then his brother commented about how nice it was have a brother in town. He mentioned how he wouldn't dare ask anyone else out on a night like that. Wolfe began to think about that observation. His brother was right. However reluctant we might be to get dressed and go out on a bad night, we don't leave a brother stranded somewhere. It then occurred to Wolfe that if we are all God's children, then all God's children have a claim upon us, and we mustn't leave any of our brothers or sisters stranded anywhere. Somewhere a house has burned down, there has been a death, or a family is destitute because unemployment benefits have been exhausted. Somewhere a brother or sister is standing on an icy street waiting for us. We are not always certain of how we can help, but the challenge to help is there. A neighbor is whoever needs our help.

The way we show that love is by our actions. For example, we show love by helping where we can. I heard about a man who joined a church in middle life. A short time later the pastor asked him to visit a crippled older gentleman who had been confined to bed and a rocking chair for many years. The man went with reluctance. To his surprise, he enjoyed the visit. But more than that, he took it upon himself to get the gentleman a much-needed wheelchair. This started a ministry. For many years thereafter this man secured scores of wheelchairs from people who didn't need them and gave them to others who did. This simple service helped deepen his faith and made his faith a living thing.

Our love for God cannot be separated from our love for God's family. In one of his last appearances to his disciples, Jesus said to Peter, "Simon son of John, do you love me?" (John 21:16). When Peter answered affirmatively, Jesus said, "Tend my sheep." Those lambs, of course, were people; and they still are: friends, relatives, hometown folks, but also refugees, homeless street people, the friendless, the hungry, and people who are different from us. When we love, we give, and the measure of our giving is the measure of our loving.

The third thing Jesus mentions is love of self. "You shall love your neighbor as (you love) yourself," he said (v. 39). There is a kind of self-love that is negative because it is self-centered. An ancient Greek myth tells about Narcissus. He was a handsome young lad who rejected all who would love him. While gazing at his own reflection in a well, he fell in love with himself. He was so totally engaged with himself that he fell into the water and drowned. What the ancient storytellers were trying to get across is that total preoccupation with self leads to destruction.

However, there is another kind of self-love that is desirable. It is called self-esteem, self-respect, and acceptance that we are persons of worth because God is our Father and we belong to God's family. In his book *Self-Esteem* (Waco, Texas: Word Books, 1982, p. 91), Robert Schuller provides a litany of what this discovery means:

> I may be young; I may be old,
> But I am somebody,
> For I am God's child.
>
> I may be educated; I may be unlettered,
> But I am somebody,

For I am God's child.

I may be black; I may be white,
But I am somebody,
For I am God's child.

I may be rich; I may be poor,
But I am somebody,
For I am God's child.
....

I may be a sinner; I may be a saint,
But I am somebody,
For Jesus is my Savior.

I am God's child!

When we know to whose family we belong, we learn to esteem ourselves correctly. The Norwegians tell a tale of a boy who found an egg in a nest while walking in the woods. He took it home and placed it with the eggs under a goose. When it hatched, what a freakish creature it was: deformed feet — unwebbed and claw-like — that made it stumble as it tried to follow the little goslings; a beak that was pointed and twisted instead of flat; its down was an ugly brown instead of light yellow; and to top it off, he made a terrible squawking sound. One day a giant eagle flew across the barnyard. The eagle swept lower and lower until the strange, awkward little bird on the ground lifted his head and pointed his crooked beak into the sky. The misfit creature then stretched his wings out and began to hobble across the yard. He flapped his wings harder and harder until the wind picked him up and carried him higher and higher. He began to soar through the clouds. He had discovered what he was: he was born an eagle! He had been trying to live like a goose.

We were born to soar. We are children of God. When we

know that, we learn to love ourselves because we love the God who made us.

Loving God, neighbor, and ourselves is not something that we perfect all at once. A friend tells of receiving a valentine card that said on the cover: "I love you terribly." Inside were the words "But I'll improve with practice." It is not an easy task to be loving persons. We are busy, we are frustrated, impatient, or too tired to try. Those we are called to love are often unlovable. Yet it is in that love triangle of God, others, and self that we find the secret of a fulfilling life on earth and a foretaste of the life to come.

Reformation Day
John 8:31-36

Being a True Disciple

> Then Jesus said to the Jews who had believed in him, "If you continue in my word, you are truly my disciples; and you will know the truth, and the truth will make you free." They answered him, "We are descendants of Abraham and have never been slaves to anyone. What do you mean by saying, 'You will be made free'?" Jesus answered them, "Very truly, I tell you, everyone who commits sin is a slave to sin. The slave does not have a permanent place in the household; the son has a place there forever. So if the Son makes you free, you will be free indeed."

I attended a church recently where the pastor was lamenting the fact that the Christian church has many members who are fans of Jesus but too few who are committed disciples. He described a fan as an enthusiastic admirer who wants to be close enough to Jesus to get all the benefits but not so close that it requires sacrifice. Fans may feel fine about repeating a prayer, attending church on the weekend, and slapping a fish emblem on their bumpers. Jesus, the pastor said, is not interested in recruiting admirers; he is seeking disciples.

Most people who call themselves Christian would probably say that they are disciples of Christ. It becomes more complicated when we try to define what we mean by "disciple." The words of Jesus found in the portion of the gospel of John that we read earlier tells of an incident in the life of Jesus that helps us to understand what a disciple is. In this situation, some Jewish people had been listening to Jesus for a while and they had become believers. We are not told what they believed, but Jesus seems to accept the fact that they were believers.

From that incident, the first thing we can say is that discipleship begins with belief. For many people, unfortunately, that is not only the first step in Christian development, it is the only step. It reduces Christianity to the lowest common denominator. To their defense such people call on the great reformer, Martin Luther, who discovered and taught that we are saved by faith. Indeed, before him the apostle Paul indicated that we are saved by God's grace through faith and not from anything we can do to earn it (Ephesians 2:8).

A few years ago an evangelistic organization announced their plan to proclaim the gospel to every person in the world who had a telephone listing. Christians everywhere were recruited and urged to take responsibility for several pages of the local telephone directory, calling the people who appeared on those pages and telling them about Jesus Christ. Somewhere along the way the idea just kind of ran out of steam. Another group of people found a passage in the Bible indicating that Jesus would return only when every person in the world had heard the gospel. They recruited people to recite to every person they met John 3:16: "God so loved the world that he gave his only Son, so that everyone who believes in him may not perish but may have eternal life." You can still occasionally see a person seated behind the goalposts at a football game holding up a placard saying "John 3:16." Maybe it does some good.

Some people may be able to say they have found God by simply saying "I believe." They may be Christians, but they are neophytes. An infant is a human being with great potential, but the infant has a long way to go before he or she will be a mature person. If there is no further growth in such a child, we speak sadly of arrested development. It is the same with regard to believers. There is a maxim that says "well begun is half done." Saying "I believe" is a good beginning, but we need to remember that the task is only half done.

In the days when men went to sea in wooden ships, experienced sailors were much in demand. Shipping companies would pay a premium for those who had sailed around Cape Horn. Recruiters, anxious to fill their quota, would ask a young applicant if he had ever been around the Horn. If the applicant said "no," the recruiter would take him into a backroom and place the horn of a steer on the floor. The agent would then tell the man to walk slowly around the horn. When that was accomplished, the recruiter would tell the young man that he qualified for the job. If anyone asked him if he'd been around the Horn, he was to say "yes." It was a shortcut, but really there is no shortcut that will give a seaman the skills he needs to be a competent sailor. Neither is there an easy way to make a neophyte Christian into a mature disciple.

The second thing we learn from this scripture is that discipleship calls for action. Apparently those new Jewish believers were not growing in the faith. We are not told all that transpired between them and Jesus, but Jesus addressed them and called for a deeper relationship. He said, in effect, "If you *continue* in my word, you are truly my disciples." He was saying that his disciples need to *abide in* or live in what he was saying. Becoming a disciple is an ongoing process. Each believer needs to grow. The newfound faith needs to deepen. A disciple is a learner. A Christian disciple seeks to learn from Jesus.

To say "I believe in God" is a beginning, but it is only a beginning. To say "I've been born again" means that one is a spiritual infant who needs to think about what it means to follow Christ. Some years ago the *Christian Century* magazine ran a series of articles titled "How My Mind Has Changed." Various theologians were invited to write articles about how their minds had changed over the years. A number of people didn't like the idea. They felt that theology meant the truth about God. To admit a change of mind had to mean a loss or even a denial of truth. For religious thinkers to change their positions would undermine the faith of believers. Even the Catholic church, during the Second Vatican Council, recognized development and revision of doctrine during its meetings. When the Council finally ended its meetings, one Catholic woman was heard to say, "Thank God that Vatican Council stopped meeting. If they'd gone on any longer, I would have died a Protestant." Growth leads to change but it is not appreciated by those who don't want to admit that change is appropriate.

Bud Freeman, in his book *You Don't Look Like a Musician*, tells of an incident out of the life of Louis Armstrong. He says that Louis Armstrong spent a lot of time walking the streets of Chicago's South Side. During one stroll he saw a crowd gathered around two street musicians. They were playing his song "Struttin' With Some Barbecue." When they finished, he walked over to them and said, "You're playing that song too slow." "How do you know?" came the reply. "I am Louis Armstrong, and that's my chorus you're playing," Armstrong answered. The next day the two minstrels had a sign next to their tin cup which read: "Pupils of Louis Armstrong." Those musicians were humorous, but incorrect. A moment with a master musician doesn't make you his pupil, and a moment spent in Jesus' school of discipleship doesn't make you a disciple. Both take a lifetime.

Discipleship is costly. Gary Player was for years a great competitor in national and international golf tournaments. People would constantly come up to him and make the same remark: "I'd give anything if I could hit a golf ball like you." Player, on one occasion, lost his patience when a spectator made that comment and replied:

> No, you wouldn't. You'd do anything to hit a golf ball like me, if it were easy! You know what you have to do to hit a golf ball like me? You've got to get up at 5:00 every morning, go out to the golf course, and hit a thousand golf balls! Your hands start bleeding, and you walk to the clubhouse and wash the blood off your hands, slap a bandage on it, and go out and hit another thousand golf balls! That's what it takes to hit a golf ball like me.
> (Jerry D. Butcher, "Just Do It!" *Clergy Journal*, February 1993, p. 11)

Becoming a disciple will also cost us something.

A few years ago someone promoted one of those fast-track evangelism programs designed to win the world to Christ quickly and easily. It involved putting a bumper sticker on your car that read "I Found It." Supposedly a person's interest would be piqued by that, and when they asked you what you found, it would open the door for you to tell them about Christ. It lost steam and eventually competitive bumper stickers showed up that said "I Never Lost It." Recognizing that becoming a mature Christian is a lifelong process, it would have been more honest if the first bumper sticker had said "I Am Finding It." According to Jesus, we are to *continue* in his word, always open to something new.

Jesus said that if his disciples continued in his word they would know the truth. I think that "continuing" in his word means we are to put into practice what we are learning. Tony Campolo (*Everything You've Heard Is Wrong* [Dallas: Word Publishing, 1992], p. 185) tells a story written by the Danish philosopher Sören Kierkegaard in which he describes a make-believe town where only ducks live. It was Sunday morning in Duckville and, as was the custom, all the ducks walked out of their houses and down the streets to the First Duckist Church. They waddled down the aisle of the church, waddled into the pews, and squatted. Shortly afterward, the duck minister took his place in the pulpit and the church service got underway. The scripture text for the morning was taken from the duck Bible and it read:

> Ducks, God has given you wings —
> you can fly.
> Ducks, because you have wings
> you can fly like eagles.
> Because God has given you wings
> no fences can confine you,
> no land animals can trap you.
> Ducks! God has given you wings!

And all the ducks said "Amen!" And then they got up and waddled home.

It is not enough to simply hear the word. The truth for us is discovered when we act on what we have heard. The deepest knowing comes through doing. Apprentices learn from watching and listening to the journeyman, but the learners accomplish something only when they put what they have learned into practice.

In his book *Miracle of Motivation* (Wheaton, Illinois: Tyndale House Publishers, 1981, pp. 4-6), George Shin tells of an incident related to him by W. Clement Stone, author of many books on motivation. One day a woman called Stone's office to complain about two of Mr. Stone's books. Mr. Stone was out, but Linda, one of his secretaries, listened to the angry woman's complaints. Apparently, the woman and her husband had bought a couple of Mr. Stone's books on the secrets of success, but the books had done them no good. The woman was still a waitress — a job she hated — and her husband was still unemployed. Mr. Stone's advice had been useless. Perceptively, Linda asked, "But what action did you take as a result of reading Mr. Stone's books?" There was silence, and then the woman answered, "I waited."

The secretary gently explained that the self-help books were written in order to motivate people to *act*. She told the woman to read the books again but to look for specific ideas upon which to act. Many months later, the woman reached Linda again. She wanted to share with Linda how helpful her advice had been. The woman had returned to school to learn office skills and already received some wonderful job offers for when she graduated. Her husband was now actively searching for a job. The problems didn't magically disappear, but the man and woman were taking positive actions in their lives. The truth of what they were told was proved by acting on what they learned.

The final thing Jesus says in this passage about true discipleship is that it makes us free. Noting how many people are hemmed in by religion, it may seem unlikely that religion can really offer freedom. Part of our confusion stems from misunderstanding what is meant by freedom. In the musical *My Fair Lady*, Professor Higgins reflects the notion of freedom held by many when he defines himself as "an ordinary man who desires nothing more than just an ordinary chance to live exactly as he likes and do precisely what he wants." In reality, there is no such absolute freedom. Even if we could do what we wanted, it would involve choices, and those choices would then limit the remaining options, for if you do *this*, you can't do *that* at the same time; if you take *this* road, you cannot also take *that* road.

A few years ago I served a church in Lancaster, California, a self-contained community up on the high desert. Most of the young people talked about moving down to Los Angeles, either for education or for a job. They looked forward to the anonymity of the big city, freedom from restraint, opportunity to do as they pleased, which was difficult in a small town. What surprised me was the number of those young people who moved back to Lancaster after trying life in the big city. Without the restraints to which they had become accustomed, life had become impossibly complicated, and far from finding freedom, many felt they were losing their freedom to become what God intended. When we are immature, we need some external restraints to guard us and rules to guide us. As we grow to maturity, some of those external restraints may be less necessary and less relevant and may be discarded by us. Even so, as old restraints are taken away new resources must be found, lest we yield to license and lose our freedom to be what we were intended to be. We need something that will give us balance.

Boundaries can actually enhance our freedom. Freedom without boundaries can cause us to lose our way. Professor Harold de Wolf, in his book *The Religious Revolt Against Reason* (New York: Harper and Brothers, 1949, pp. 17-18), tells of an experience that describes the panic of people who lose their point of reference. He went swimming one night with a friend in the Atlantic. The water was full of phosphorescent light and every time a wave broke it showered the night with brilliance. He said he felt as if he were immersed in a fireworks display. Then, having gone out further than he intended, he looked up to the sky to get his bearings. But the sky was like the water — full of the spectacular confusion of the northern lights. No star was visible. Then panic overtook him, for in all that glittering display there was no fixed reality. He could not tell the way to shore. He started back with a helpless terror engulfing him. His freedom, which was unbounded, threatened to destroy him. He learned that freedom is found in knowing where we are and who we are. To know where we are we need some boundaries.

I think one of the important truths Jesus reveals to his disciples is that the fullness of life is found in service. At first that doesn't sound like freedom. Someone told me about the life of Marian Preminger. She was born in Hungary in 1913, raised in a castle with her aristocratic family, and surrounded by maids, tutors, governesses, butlers, and chauffeurs. Her grandmother, who lived with them, insisted that whenever they traveled they should take their own linens because she felt it was beneath their dignity to sleep between sheets used by common people.

While attending school in Vienna, Marian met a handsome doctor. They fell in love, eloped, and married when she was only eighteen. The marriage lasted only a year and she returned to Vienna to begin her life as an actress. While auditioning for a play she met a brilliant young German director, Otto Preminger. They fell in love and soon married. They went to America soon thereafter, where he began his career as a movie director. Marian got caught up in the glamour, fast life, and superficial excitement of Hollywood and soon began to live a sordid life. Her husband divorced her. She returned to Europe to live the life of a socialite in Paris.

In 1948 she read that Albert Schweitzer, a man she read about as a little girl, was making one of his periodic trips to Europe and was staying in the town of Gunsbach. She went to visit him, he invited her to dinner, and by the end of the day she discovered what her life had been lacking. He invited her to come to Africa to work in his hospital. She went and there in Lambarene the girl born in a castle and spoiled by luxury became a servant and found herself. She changed bandages, bathed babies, fed lepers, and in the process became free. In her autobiography, *All I Ever Wanted Was Everything*, she acknowledged that she couldn't *get* the "everything" that would satisfy and give meaning until she was able to *give* everything. When she died in 1979 her obituary carried her own words, in which she said: "Albert Schweitzer said there are two classes of people in this world — the helpers and the non-helpers. I am a helper." What she did was of her own free will. The truth took up residence in her and freed her to be able to serve. "If you continue in my word," said Jesus, "you are truly my disciples; and you will know the truth, and the truth will make you free" (vv. 31-32).

All Saints Day
Matthew 5:1-12

Hallelujah!
Come On, Get Happy

When Jesus saw the crowds, he went up the mountain; and after he sat down, his disciples came to him. Then he began to speak, and taught them, saying: "Blessed are the poor in spirit, for theirs is the kingdom of heaven. Blessed are those who mourn, for they will be comforted. Blessed are the meek, for they will inherit the earth. Blessed are those who hunger and thirst for righteousness, for they will be filled. Blessed are the merciful, for they will receive mercy. Blessed are the pure in heart, for they will see God. Blessed are the peacemakers, for they will be called children of God. Blessed are those who are persecuted for righteousness' sake, for theirs is the kingdom of heaven. Blessed are you when people revile you and persecute you and utter all kinds of evil against you falsely on my account. Rejoice and be glad, for your reward is great in heaven, for in the same way they persecuted the prophets who were before you."

At the entrance to Disneyland is a sign that reads: "Disneyland — the happiest place on earth." Millions of people have come from all over the world to visit and partake of the happiness it was designed to create. Happiness is something that humans seek naturally. We are all on a pleasure hunt. We Americans even wrote the pursuit of happiness into our constitutional rights. Yet the more earnestly we pursue happiness, the more elusive it becomes.

June Callwood, in her article "One Sure Way to Happiness" (*Reader's Digest*, October 1974), tells us that the historian Will Durant wrote how he looked for happiness in knowledge and found only disillusionment. He then sought happiness in travel and found weariness; in wealth and found discord and worry. He looked for happiness in his writing and was only fatigued. One day he saw a woman waiting in a train station with a sleeping child in her arms. A man descended from a train and came over and gently kissed the woman and then the baby, very softly so as not to waken him. The family drove off and left Durant with a stunning realization that happiness is a by-product of our simplest activities.

Jesus goes beyond Durant and indicates in this Matthew passage that happiness is possible even in the midst of negative experiences. If that is possible, it is certainly something we need to hear — we who must deal with the loss of loved ones, the loss of a job, or the loss of property. What do these words of Jesus mean?

For one thing, from the illustrations he used, I think Jesus was pointing out that happiness is related to the attitude we bring to the experience. "Blessed," he said, "are the poor in spirit..." The word that is translated "blessed" is translated as "happy" in many of the more modern translations. Those translators wanted to use a word that would be more in keeping with the way we speak today. I will follow their lead and use "happy" in place of "blessed."

Somehow we have been taught to believe that to be happy we need to be in control. I saw a cartoon in which a fellow was bowed in prayer. He was saying, "God, can you help me, but sort of make it look like I did it all myself?" If we can't *be* in control we certainly want it to *look like* we are in control. But to be spiritually poor means to recognize that there are many areas in which we are not in control. Robert Schuller, in his book *The Be-Happy Attitudes* (Waco, Texas: Word Books, 1985, pp. 33-34), tells of being raised in an Iowa farm family where there was always plenty of home-baked bread, butter, pies, and other desserts. As a consequence, he says, he has always had a problem with weight. He eventually decided to eat only lean meats, vegetables, and fresh fruits for dessert. One night a few years ago someone took him to dinner and raved about the fresh warm bread as he spread it with butter. Schuller had some. "You must try the steak with bernaise sauce," said the host. Schuller followed the advice. After the steak, the host continued, "They make the best pie here, with a chocolate crust. You can't pass it by." Schuller had a piece. He calculated in that one meal he took in about 3,000 calories. That night he was depressed and filled with remorse that he did not have the strength to get rid of his fat. He says he prayed asking Jesus to help him. As long as he felt that he could safely eat a little here and a little there and still remain in control, he was doomed. But when he cried out for help and admitted that he couldn't control his appetite by himself, he was freed from his addiction. Alcoholics Anonymous operates on the same premise. Persons addicted to alcohol find help only when they acknowledge their own helplessness and reach for help beyond themselves. Happiness can come in the midst of our misery when we acknowledge that we have a need and we are spiritually poor.

"Happy are those who are meek," says Jesus. The word "meek" means humble. We have been taught by our experiences that it is important to be right. In a *Peanuts* cartoon Peppermint Patty says, "I need some good advice, Roy. What do you do when something you had really counted on doesn't happen? This thing I really believed would happen didn't happen. What do I do?" "Well," says Roy, "you could admit you were wrong." "Yeah," says Peppermint Patty, "besides that, I mean." As long as we nurture our pride, it keeps us from growing, learning, and becoming all we are capable of becoming.

Fritz Widmeyer, a United Methodist minister in New York, seems to have captured the meaning of Jesus' words in a letter he wrote to the editor of the *United Methodist Reporter* (date unavailable):

> When I was in college and seminary, I discovered that I was only an average student. And now I've discovered that I am only an average minister. There are better preachers than I am; better teachers, better visitors, better administrators. I keep making dumb mistakes and sometimes I don't know how to rectify them. I can only beg forgiveness and promise not to do that again. However, I've also discovered that my talents, limited though they may be, are useful. I have a place in the church and the world. No, I'll never be Number One, but that's okay as long as I do the best I can with what God has given me.

He found happiness in his humility. Those who are not filled with pride and concerned with who gets the credit can be very useful in extending Christ's kingdom. Their happiness comes from being useful.

"Happy are those who hunger and thirst for righteousness," says Jesus. These are people who want to do God's will. We have been subjected to the idea that happiness involves being able to do pretty much as we please with little concern for how it affects others. I recall a line in the movie *Three Days of the Condor* that describes many people in today's world. Robert Redford shakes his head as he confronts a CIA bureaucrat and says, "You guys think that not getting caught in a lie is the same thing as telling the truth!" The comment could be applied to much of the business world or any other sector of life about as accurately as it could be applied to the CIA. Much of modern American society decides whether or not a thing is wrong by trying to figure out if they are likely to get caught and not what effect it will have on others. They are concerned only about their own will, not God's will.

Over and over Jesus taught and demonstrated that God's will for us involves helping others and that in our helping we find happiness. In his book *Generous People* (Nashville, Tennessee: Abingdon Press, 1992), Eugene Grimm reports the testimony of a woman who was standing in a long line of people waiting in the snow outside a funeral home as they sought the opportunity to pay their last respects to Walter, a neighbor who had died.

> "I only met him once," commented the young woman shivering from cold, "but he changed my life. I came to town with my husband and three children. I hadn't been here three weeks when my husband took off and left me and the kids alone. I was so scared I thought I'd die. I was unskilled and hadn't planned to work until the kids were older. One of my neighbors called Walter on the telephone. Walter sent word that he had a job for me the next week. He also offered an apartment where my children and I could live rent-free. It was four months before I could even begin to pay rent.
>
> "Two years later, I went to make arrangements for payments on back rent, and you know what he said? He looked over the top of his reading glasses and said, 'Thank you but I never intended you to pay for those months. You just go out there and find somebody in need, and help them.' That is exactly what I did. I asked my pastor if he could suggest someone who needed help. And it felt so good to give instead of receive, I just keep on helping them. Walter taught me how good it feels to give."

She learned the happiness of focusing on others.

"Happy are the pure in heart," says Jesus. Purity of heart means sincerity, having unmixed motives. I read recently that the Iroquois Indians attributed divinity to developmentally challenged children. They gave them a place of honor in the tribe and treated them as gods. It was felt that in their lack of self-centeredness, they were a transparent window into the Great Spirit. It is interesting that in their ancient culture those early Native American people learned to think of people without mixed motives as divine. Jesus says those without mixed motives, those whose hearts are pure, will see God. Those without mixed motives find happiness because they have no hidden agenda, they are genuinely pleased with the advancement of others, and they have no secret resentment that the interests of others have been advanced. They are made happy by the good fortune of others.

Not only do these words of Jesus suggest that happiness is related to attitude, they suggest that it is also the result of certain actions. Jesus says, "Happy are those who mourn." It seems unlikely to us that happiness and mourning go together. Certainly we would not expect one who is mourning a loss to feel happy, but mourning touches the deepest that is within us and helps us to identify with others, to be compassionate. In *The Human Comedy* (New York: Harcourt Brace and Company, 1966), William Saroyan wrote:

> Unless a man has pity he is inhuman and not yet truly a man, for out of pity comes the balm which heals. Only good men weep. If a man has not yet wept at the world's pain he is less than the dirt he walks upon because dirt will nourish seed, root, stalk, leaf, and flower, but the spirit of a man without pity is barren and will bring forth nothing.

When we mourn, we learn to have compassion for others.

A class in seminary was discussing Jesus' parable of the Good Samaritan. A young student confessed an incident, of which he was not very proud, which had occurred the evening before. He was hurrying through the door of his apartment headed for the laundry room with a basket of dirty clothes. He scarcely noticed the neighbor lady who lived alone across the hall. She was struggling to get a grocery sack of trash up a flight of steps to the trash container. She was quite crippled and put the sack down on each step as she labored to get both feet up on that step. It was an awkward, painful process, but as he didn't know her well he paid no attention. It wasn't until he was loading the washing machine that it occurred to him that his behavior completely betrayed his sense of who he was as a Christian. He confessed to his class that he was ashamed of his failure to act on behalf of another. It is safe to say that had that student ever known such infirmity or experienced such hardship, his concern or mourning would have been sharper and more alert. One of the godly uses of our own sorrows, hurts, and sufferings is the way in which we can thereby be trained to understand and mourn the hardships of others.

Jesus goes on to say, "Happy are the merciful." Something inside of us prefers revenge over mercy for those who have wronged us. The nineteenth-century German writer Heinrich Heine once wrote:

> My nature is the most peaceful in the world. All I ask is a simple cottage, a decent bed, good food, some flowers in front of my window, and a few trees beside my door. Then if God wanted to make me wholly happy, He would let me enjoy the spectacle of six or seven of my enemies dangling from those trees. I would forgive them all wrongs they have done me — forgive them from the bottom of my heart, for we must forgive our enemies. But not until they are hanged!
> (quoted in "Revenge," Resource Service, 3/89-4/89)

One cannot help but feel that whatever satisfaction Heine would have received from such a sight, it would not have produced any long-term happiness.

It is when we return good for evil that we show whose people we are. There is a stunning picture of forgiveness in *The Great Hunger* (Whitefish, Montana: Kessinger Publishing Co., 2004) by Johan Bojer. The lead character, Peer Holm, had a rude and crude neighbor with a vicious dog. One day, even though Peer pleaded with the neighbor to keep the dog chained to no avail, the huge beast attacked and killed Peer's small daughter. The dog was killed by the townspeople, and thereafter the village ostracized and shunned Peer's neighbor. In the spring, when the neighbor plowed his field, the merchants in the little village refused to sell him any grain. His field lay bare. One moonlit night, however, Peer took a half bushel of his own grain to his neighbor's field and sowed it. When the crops grew in the neighbor's field and there was a bare spot in Peer Holm's field, the townspeople could see what had happened. "Why did you do it?" they asked Peer. He answered, "I did it in order that God might exist in our community." What Peer knew was that in the long run happiness lay not in revenge, but in mercy and forgiveness.

"Happy are the peacemakers," continues Jesus. Contemporary wisdom advises us to mind our own business and let others look out for themselves. When someone else has a problem, the rest of us feel we will be a lot happier if we don't get involved. But the reality is that we cannot have peace if others do not have justice. Justice works on the principle of fairness for all. Where the rights of others are ignored, abused, violated, or taken away, the seeds of bitterness and hostility are sown and there will not be peace for anyone.

Peacemaking means getting involved in the struggle for justice and making that struggle our own, even if it temporarily unsettles our peace. As Harriet Beecher Stowe sat through long nights in her home in Ohio watching the struggles of a dying child, she began to think of slave mothers who were parted from their children by slavery. There was born within her the desire to move the conscience of the country to end slavery. She set about to write *Uncle Tom's Cabin* to illustrate the evils of slavery. She saw all people as children of God and recognized that as long as the well-being of one part of the family is based upon the misery of another part, there cannot be happiness for either part. Happiness is the result of certain actions.

One more thing these words of Jesus suggest is that our happiness is not dictated by our circumstances. He illustrates this by saying, "Happy are those who are persecuted for righteousness' sake." Righteousness means doing what God requires. Most of us have learned to do what is expedient:

don't make waves, blend in, go with the flow.

To act on principle certainly can be costly. President John F. Kennedy, in his book *Profiles in Courage* (New York: Harper, 1955), relates the story of Edmund G. Ross, the senator from Kansas whose vote back in 1868 decided the impeachment trial of President Andrew Johnson. Johnson courageously tried to carry out Abraham Lincoln's policies of reconciliation after the Civil War. The mood of the country, however, was to impeach the untactful Tennessean who had succeeded to the highest office of the land only by the course of an assassin's bullet. The House of Representatives speedily passed the articles of impeachment, and it seemed the Senate would handily amass the two-thirds vote necessary for conviction. It was thought that Senator Ross, who had an expressed dislike for President Johnson, would vote for the president's removal. And if he had followed his likes and dislikes, he probably would have. But the obscure senator from Kansas searched his soul for the right thing to do. To the dismay of most of his colleagues, and the majority of his supporters in his home state, he voted against impeachment. "I looked down into my open grave..." he said, but he did what he thought was right even if it meant his political death — which it did.

It doesn't sound like the decision produced happiness for Ross, but he later wrote: "Millions cursing me today will bless me tomorrow for having saved the country from the greatest peril through which it has ever passed, though none but God can ever know the struggle that it has cost me." The decision to do what he felt was right was costly, but there was the happiness of knowing he had done what he felt was right.

What are the circumstances that we face? The loss of someone who gave life meaning? The loss of a job that provided for home and family and gave us fulfillment? The loss of health and independence? Are we to pretend that these things are unimportant — that they don't affect our happiness?

These words of Jesus do not suggest our circumstances do not cause us pain. If we are human, if we love someone or enjoy something, we will eventually know loss and that will produce pain. If there is anything called happiness, it will be in spite of our difficulties and not because we have managed to avoid them. Some of our difficulties will create happiness in the long run because they will change our attitude from focus on ourselves to focus on others. Some of our difficulties will create happiness because they will cause us to act on behalf of others. Some of our difficulties will create happiness only when we recognize that God has a plan for the world, which has been advanced a little because we have sought to identify with it.

In every one of these beatitudes Jesus concludes that God will have the last word, but he also promises that that word will be good. Therein lays our hope.

Proper 26
Pentecost 21
Ordinary Time 31
Matthew 23:1-12

The Real Thing

> Then Jesus said to the crowds and to his disciples, "The scribes and the Pharisees sit on Moses' seat; therefore, do whatever they teach you and follow it; but do not do as they do, for they do not practice what they teach. They tie up heavy burdens, hard to bear, and lay them on the shoulders of others; but they themselves are unwilling to lift a finger to move them. They do all their deeds to be seen by others; for they make their phylacteries broad and their fringes long. They love to have the place of honor at banquets and the best seats in the synagogues, and to be greeted with respect in the marketplaces, and to have people call them rabbi. But you are not to be called rabbi, for you have one teacher, and you are all students. And call no one your father on earth, for you have one Father — the one in heaven. Nor are you to be called instructors, for you have one instructor, the Messiah. The greatest among you will be your servant. All who exalt themselves will be humbled, and all who humble themselves will be exalted."

Mahatma Gandhi of India is alleged to have said, "If I had ever met someone who was a genuine Christian, I would have become one immediately." It is a stinging judgment of Christians. At the same time, it challenges every Christian to examine the genuineness of his or her walk and witness. We need to ask ourselves: "How authentic, how credible is my demonstration of the Christian life?"

In our scripture lesson for today Jesus criticizes certain characteristics of the Pharisees, a sectarian group within Judaism. Because Jesus was so often in conflict with the

Pharisees, we are apt to think of them as enemies of the good. Nothing could be further from the truth. They were pillars of the community, ardent patriots, and respected in the community as citizens of highest character. The Pharisees probably got their name from a word meaning "separated." They took the laws of Moses and the religion of Israel very seriously. In attempting to fulfill what they felt were the requirements of their religion, their lives became very complicated and uncomfortable. In order to fulfill as many of the requirements as possible, they found it necessary to avoid the contamination of others who did not keep the religious laws as meticulously as they did; so they separated themselves from the ordinary business of life and from ordinary people as well — hence the name. They considered it a matter of defilement to talk to, do business with, and be hospitable toward anyone who did not observe the same ritualistic requirements.

The Pharisees were not bad people. Others in the community thought of them as virtuous and that was their own estimate of themselves as well. Jesus called attention to several characteristics of the Pharisees in order to teach his followers to conduct themselves differently.

The first thing Jesus criticized in the Pharisees was a lack of authenticity. He said the Pharisees did not practice what they preached. They could talk the talk, but they didn't walk the walk. They carefully studied the Ten Commandments, but they felt that the commandments were not specific enough; so they developed 613 religious requirements, hoping to cover every eventuality. They were meticulous about religious observances, but what motivated many of them was the notoriety and respect that their observances brought to them.

I read about an elegant party that was being held in one of those big English country houses. Often after dinner at such parties, people would give recitations, sing, or use whatever talent they had to entertain the company. One evening a famous actor was among the guests. Some say that it was Charles Laughton. When it came his turn to perform, he recited the 23rd Psalm, perhaps the most beloved Psalm in the Psalter: "The Lord is my shepherd. I shall not want." His rendition was magnificent and there was much applause.

At the end of the evening someone noticed an older woman dozing in a corner. She was deaf as a post and had missed most of what had been going on, but she was urged to get up and recite something. So she stood up and in her quavering old voice she started "The Lord is my Shepherd" and went on to the end of the Psalm, not knowing it had been recited once before that evening. When she finished there were tears in many eyes. Later, one of the guests approached the famous actor and said, "You recited that Psalm absolutely superbly. It was incomparable. So why were we so moved by that funny little lady?" He replied, "I know the Psalm. She knows the shepherd" (Madeleine L'Engle, *The Rock That Is Higher* [reported in *Lection Aid*, Vol. 4, No. 4], p. 22).

By his criticism of the Pharisees, Jesus was urging his followers to be authentic and make sure that their actions conformed to their words.

The second thing Jesus does in this passage is to remind us that a principal characteristic of his followers is service. He says, "The greatest among you will be your servant." The Pharisees whom Jesus criticized wanted to be great so they could *be* served. Jesus' followers are told that, in his estimation, greatness comes from *rendering* service, even something as small as giving a person a cup of cold water (Matthew 10:42).

When we help a needy person, when we offer food to the hungry and drink to the thirsty, we are actually serving in the spirit of Jesus. When we care for the forgotten of our society as Jesus did, we are actually demonstrating the call of Jesus to render service. What we do for others has eternal consequences. Leo Tolstoy told a beautiful story about a cobbler named Martin. In a dream, Jesus promised Martin, "Tomorrow I will visit you." When he woke up in the morning he was excited. Jesus would pay a visit to him sometime during the day. He swept the shop clean, prepared a delicious meal, and waited for the visit.

In the morning a hungry, exhausted child came to his shop, so Martin fed her and let her rest for a while. At midday an old lady happened by. The woman was cold and shivering. Martin gave her a warm shawl and she went on her way. Then in the afternoon, a barefooted beggar came to his door, and Martin gave him a pair of shoes. But Jesus did not come. When Martin went to bed that night he was disappointed.

That night Jesus once again appeared to him in a dream. "Lord, why did you not visit me today?" Martin asked in all sincerity. Jesus then replied, "Martin, three times I visited you: first as a little child, then as an old woman, and finally as a beggar." Martin discovered that in serving others we serve the Lord (Piero Ferrucci, *Inevitable Grace* [Los Angeles: Jeremy P. Tarcher, Inc., 1990], pp. 90-91).

To practice our religion is to serve our fellow humans, not to show off our religion. Charles Kuralt, the television commentator, told about Pat Shannon Baker, a young white woman, mother of three children, who lived in Reno, Nevada. The night Martin Luther King was killed, Pat Baker was sitting up late, thinking "I have to do something about this." Pat often had passed a weedy vacant lot in a black neighborhood on her way to work each day, and she wondered why the city hadn't turned it into a park. She went to her city councilman to see what could be done to convert that vacant land into a park. The councilman spoke of the strained budget and the difficulty of passing a bond issue. It would take years to get through all the red tape. Pat didn't want to wait for all that. She then went to garden supply houses, cement companies, surveyors, the heads of construction unions, and tough-minded contractors she had never met before. Pretty soon, her idea became everyone's idea.

At 7:30 on a Friday morning, in a town not famous for early risers, a crowd began to gather at the vacant lot. By 8:30, 2,000 tons of donated topsoil was being spread by front-end loaders operated by heavy equipment operators who were not used to working for free. They were working for free that morning.

A school custodian, an unemployed teenager, a roofer, and a garage mechanic began working together. A junior high school kid, who was assigned to saw two-by-fours, sawed all day in the hot sun and did so as if his life depended on it. A little girl carried water to the workers. Coast Guardsmen, Marines, and Seabees came to help. Cement was laid for a double tennis court and smoothed out by noon. A basketball court was in before the sun went down. Dozens of people worked all night.

Saturday morning a crowd of several hundred showed up for work, black and white, young and old. They sodded the lawn Saturday night and turned on the sprinkler system Sunday morning. By Sunday afternoon the park was finished, with two walks and grass, basketball and tennis courts, and trees and benches. One person with a sense of commitment brought the community together. More than twenty years later the grass was still neatly mowed. The trees were tall and leafy. In the shade of the trees people were sitting on benches and talking. Some kids who hadn't been born in 1968 were practicing shots on the basketball court. One person was prepared to serve and scores of people enlisted (Charles Kuralt, *A Life on the Road* [New York: G.P. Putnam's Sons, 1990], pp. 134-135).

Jesus seems to be aware that even something as noble as service can be corrupted by pride, so he tells his followers that "all who exalt themselves will be humbled, and all who humble themselves will be exalted" (v. 12).

As a student at Oxford University, John Wesley, the founder of Methodism, along with his brother Charles and other friends shared in what they called The Holy Club. The club members practiced spiritual disciplines and devoted themselves to good works in order to render themselves worthy of God. Wesley would come away from the prisons he and the others had visited holding his nose because of the smell and thinking to himself, "God must be very proud of me for visiting these derelicts." In spite of Wesley's satisfaction with himself, God remained strangely remote. It wasn't until Wesley himself experienced God's acceptance that he could get over focusing on himself and challenge England to do something about the inhumane treatment of prisoners. The time came when he was no longer concerned about how spiritual he was in God's sight, but instead, in gratitude for God's saving love, he determined to show Christ's love by serving those in need. Pride about how good we are can separate us from God.

Jesus urges us to be wary of the human tendency to point to our own good works in such a way that we detract from what has been accomplished. There's a story told of a well-known Christian businessman who was visiting a church and as a matter of courtesy he was asked to bring a word of greeting. Unfortunately, he got rather carried away in the process and went on to tell the congregation of all the wonderful things he had done for the Lord.

> "I have a large house, a fine family, a successful business, and good reputation. I have enough money to do whatever I want, and I'm able to support some Christian ministries very generously. Many of those ministries want me to be on their board of directors. I have almost unlimited opportunities. Most people would love to change places with me. What more could God give me?" As he paused for effect, a voice shouted from the

back of the auditorium, "How about a good dose of humility?" (reported in Pastors' Pulpit Resource Service, Sept/Oct 1991)

It is no wonder that Jesus taught us to do good works in secret and leave it to God to provide the reward (Matthew 6:4).

I close with this: Some years ago, while he was still the basketball coach for UCLA, I was at a gathering where Larry Brown was describing the members of his team. While he was glad to have star players, his highest praise was for those players who made other team members look good. They didn't need to make all the points. They set up others. As a result, the whole team benefited.

In these verses from the gospel of Matthew, Jesus is calling us to a life in which what we do is consistent with what we say, and what we do is to serve others without regard for who gets the credit.

Proper 27
Pentecost 22
Ordinary Time 32
Matthew 25:1-13

Always Ready

Then the kingdom of heaven will be like this. Ten bridesmaids took their lamps and went to meet the bridegroom. Five of them were foolish, and five were wise. When the foolish took their lamps, they took no oil with them; but the wise took flasks of oil with their lamps. As the bridegroom was delayed, all of them became drowsy and slept. But at midnight there was a shout, "Look! Here is the bridegroom! Come out to meet him." Then all those bridesmaids got up and trimmed their lamps. The foolish said to the wise, "Give us some of your oil, for our lamps are going out." But the wise replied, "No! there will not be enough for you and for us; you had better go to the dealers and buy some for yourselves." And while they went to buy it, the bridegroom came, and those who were ready went with him into the wedding banquet; and the door was shut. Later the other bridesmaids came also, saying, "Lord, lord, open to us." But he replied, "Truly I tell you, I do not know you." Keep awake therefore, for you know neither the day nor the hour.

Some literature students at the University of Chicago once asked Ernest Hemingway what hidden meanings were in his stories. He merely shrugged and said he didn't know of any and that they could make of his stories whatever they wanted.

Biblical scholars seem to have a similar attitude toward the story Jesus told about ten bridesmaids who went out to meet a bridegroom. Five of the maidens neglected to bring extra oil for their lamps; they are called the foolish maidens. Five remembered to bring extra oil; they are the wise maidens. The bridegroom is delayed and all the bridesmaids fall asleep. When a crier proclaims that the bridegroom has arrived, all ten bridesmaids wake up and rush to their lamps. During the long night the lamps had run out of oil. This was no problem to those who had thought to bring extra oil. Those who had not brought extra oil tried to borrow from those who had. They were denied and had to run to the stores to try to find a merchant who would open up and sell them oil. Meanwhile, the bridegroom arrived and the parable ends with those who are prepared going into the feast. The door was closed and those not prepared were left outside.

Some see this as a message of warning by Jesus to the Jews of his day who should have been prepared for his coming but were not. Others see it as a parable of Jesus that was reworked by Matthew to be used in the conflict between first-century Christians and hostile Jews. Still others see it as a reference by Jesus to his second coming, at which time those who are ready will join Jesus and those who are not ready will be shut out. While any or all of these interpretations may be correct, we need to remember that a parable makes one point. We do not need to make it into an allegory in which every person and every action stands for a particular person or situation. It is more important to apply this parable to ourselves than to limit its application to people in the past or the future.

The first thing this parable says to me is that whatever you want to do or to be, there is a need to prepare. All ten bridesmaids had prepared their lamps so they would be able to march in procession accompanying the bridegroom, and no doubt the bride, to their new home. When the group arrived at the couple's new home, there would be a celebration, and though the girls were not part of the official wedding party, they would be welcome at the festivities because of the part they played in lighting the wedding parade.

We are apt to attribute someone's success in a field to certain natural gifts possessed by the successful person, but more often success is a result of preparation. For example, in sports, Wayne Gretzky is seen as one of the greatest hockey players of all time. In the 1980s he won the National Hockey League's Most Valuable Player award an unprecedented nine out of a possible ten times. It took the previous holder of the goal-scoring record 26 years to set the record. Gretzky did it in 15. You wouldn't know it to look at him. He is smaller and lighter than the average hockey player. He didn't skate particularly fast or gracefully. His shot was not a real burner, and on strength tests administered to each member of his team, Gretzky always placed dead last. What made him such a winner was practice in season and out of season, especially practicing unusual shots like bouncing the puck off the side boards or the side of the net to a teammate. He practiced those shots so much that he could do them in any direction. He may have had a gift, but he was also the best prepared member of his team.

Success in literature is another field that requires preparation. As a schoolboy I learned that Abraham Lincoln wrote the marvelous Gettysburg Address on the back of an envelope as he rode on the train to the dedication of the military cemetery at Gettysburg. An official who accompanied the president said that he did no writing on the trip. His address was delivered on November 19. However, when he spoke informally to a crowd on the White House lawn four months earlier, he said: "How long ago is it? Eighty-odd years since, on the Fourth of July, for the first time in the history of the world, a nation... declared, as a self-evident truth that all nations are created equal." These are phrases that appear in the Gettysburg Address, showing that more than four months before the Gettysburg Address Lincoln was already sharpening the classic wording contained in the speech. Lincoln had oil in his lamp. He'd been storing it for months, and when the occasion arose he was ready for the task. Successful people may have gifts that contribute to their success, but even they have to prepare.

The second thing this parable says to me is that as we prepare to reach our goal, we must also prepare for the unexpected. In the parable the bridegroom's coming was delayed. Five of the bridesmaids prepared for that eventuality; they brought extra oil. There's a story told about a Cornish farmer who had difficulty keeping a hired man because his farm was located on the west coast of England, where storms roared in off the Atlantic. It was a miserable place to be. The farmer looked and looked for help. Finally, a man came and applied for the job. He was a little fellow. He didn't look very strong and appeared to be past middle age. He looked like he could be on his last leg. But he was the only person the farmer had found.

The farmer asked him, "Are you a good helper to a farmer?" The man answered in his Cornish accent, "I can sleep when the wind blows." When the farmer said, "I don't understand," the little fellow repeated, "I can sleep when the wind blows." The farmer didn't know what that meant, but he took the man on because he desperately needed help. The man worked well around the farm and seemed to be effective. Then one night the farmer could hear the wind kicking up and beginning to blow. He got out of bed, lit the lantern, went to the barn where the hired man was sleeping and shook him awake. "The storm is coming and the wind is howling," the farmer shouted. "We have to do something fast." The hired man looked at him and said, "No, sir, I told you, I can sleep when the wind blows." The farmer went outside and saw that all the haystacks had been covered by tarpaulins, all the chickens were in coops, all the cows were in the barn, all of the things that could have blown away were secured and all doors and shutters closed. Indeed, the hired man could sleep when the wind blew. He was prepared when it came to regular farm work, and he was able to deal with a change of circumstances.

There are some preparations that can't be put off until the last minute. It's too late for a student to begin preparing for an exam when the day of examination has come. It is too late to acquire a skill when a job comes along that requires us to already have that skill. In the theater, a relatively unknown actress may be given a small part but also be assigned to be the understudy for the leading female. Broadway lore is filled with stories of actresses who were called upon to fill in for the leading actress and who did so well that they became leading actresses themselves. They prepared themselves in advance.

It is the same in our relationship with God. It is told of Queen Mary of Orange that when she was dying, her chaplain came to speak to her about her relationship with God. "My friend," she answered gently, "I did not leave such an important matter till this hour." Circumstances can change quickly. The day of death is not the time to begin thinking about the place of God in our lives.

Another thing this parable says to me is that there are some things in life that can't be borrowed from others. The five bridesmaids without extra oil could not get by on the preparations of others. When they tried to borrow oil, they were refused. They would have to go back into the town to see if they could find a merchant who would open his store to sell them oil.

It is that way in many situations in life. For example, we cannot get by on somebody else's education. We may have gifted teachers who are willing to share their education, but the student must take responsibility for assimilating what is taught. Jesse Jackson, speaking about the education of inner-city children, said, "We keep saying that Johnny can't read because he's deprived, hungry, and discriminated against.... The reason Johnny can't read well is that Johnny doesn't practice reading" (quoted in *Pulpit Resource*, Vol. 9, No. 3, p. 45).

Personal responsibility is also important to the development of one's spiritual life. As I was calling on people in the community who had attended our church, I met a man who told me that he had been a Methodist all his life. He was born a Methodist, he said. In fact, his great-grandfather was a Methodist preacher. When I asked him how he and his family happened to attend our church, he acknowledged that it was actually his wife and children who attended. He couldn't make it. It turned out that he hadn't made it to church for years. In fact, the last time there was a genuine decision for Christ in his family, it was made by his great-grandfather. On the strength of that decision rested the assessment that his family was Methodist for generations. As lovingly as possible I tried to point out to him that each person has to decide for himself to follow Christ, and after that decision, a person may decide to identify with one church or another. He was not ready to go that far. The visit ended with an invitation for him to come and worship with us. He did not do so.

Several years later I received a letter from him from out-of-state, telling me that he made a decision to follow Christ and he and his family were now active in a church in their new community. He acknowledged that he had been angry with me, but he now saw the importance of taking responsibility for one's own spiritual development. He was no longer content with borrowed religion.

The fourth thing this parable says to me is that in every field opportunities pass. When the members of the wedding party arrived at the bridegroom's house, all those who accompanied him were invited in and the door was shut. This doesn't necessarily suggest that the girls who weren't ready were lost. They suffered disappointment because they could not participate in the wedding festivities. There would be other weddings and other parties, but this one was closed to them because they were not ready.

As I have traveled around the world by ship in recent years I have seen large shipping containers in most ports with the name Hanjin Transportation Company written on the sides. I asked a port agent whose company that was, and I was told an interesting story of a man named Cho Choong Hoon, known as Harry to Westerners. Sometime after the liberation of Korea from Japanese control in 1945, Harry was driving along a country road in his truck when he noticed a jeep that was stalled on the side of the road. Harry stopped to offer a hand and helped to get the vehicle started. One of the jeep's passengers, a U.S. Army officer, thanked Harry for his help and told Harry to look him up sometime. Harry did that and the acquaintanceship bloomed into a contract to haul supplies for the U.S. Army. Prior to and during the Korean War, Harry's Hanjin Transportation Company earned tens of millions of dollars, and his financial empire, Hanjin Group, became a conglomerate that now owns Korean Air Lines. Harry saw an opportunity and seized it before it disappeared. He knew what it meant to "seize the day."

In a nursery where trees and plants are sold in London, Ontario, Canada, there is a sign in the tree section that reads: "The best time to plant a tree was 25 years ago..." a sobering jolt that reminds one that trees take a long time to mature. Some oak trees, for example, are sixty years old before they bear any acorns. But that isn't the whole story of that sign in the Canadian nursery. The complete message is: "The best time to plant a tree was 25 years ago. The second best time is today." That sign is a reminder that the opportunity is still open. A tree can still be planted, in spite of the squandered opportunities of 25 years ago. The door is still open, and as long as it is, there is still opportunity to act.

The parable of the ten bridesmaids reminds us that to reach our goal we need to prepare, we need to be ready to deal with the unexpected, we need to rely on our own personal experiences, and we need to act when the opportunity presents itself because opportunities pass. Shakespeare expressed this very well:

> There is a tide in the affairs of men
> Which, taken at the flood, Leads on to fortune.
> Omitted, all the voyage of their life
> Is bound in shallows and in miseries
> On such a full sea are we now afloat
> And we must take the current when it serves
> Or lose our ventures.
> (*Julius Caesar*, Act IV, scene iii)

Jesus reminds us of all this in the conclusion of this parable when he says: "Keep awake therefore, for you know neither the day nor the hour" (v. 13).

Proper 28
Pentecost 23
Ordinary Time 33
Matthew 25:14-30

Talented People

For it is as if a man, going on a journey, summoned his slaves and entrusted his property to them; to one he gave five talents, to another two, to another one, to each according to his ability. Then he went away. The one who had received the five talents went off at once and traded with them, and made five more talents. In the same way, the one who had the two talents made two more talents. But the one who had received the one talent went off and dug a hole in the ground and hid his master's money. After a long time the master of those slaves came and settled accounts with them. Then the one who had received the five talents came forward, bringing five more talents, saying, "Master, you handed over to me five talents; see, I have made five more talents." His master said to him, "Well done, good and trustworthy slave; you have been trustworthy in a few things, I will put you in charge of many things; enter into the joy of your master." And the one with the two talents also came forward, saying, "Master, you handed over to me two talents; see, I have made two more talents." His master said to him, "Well done, good and trustworthy slave; you have been trustworthy in a few things, I will put you in charge of many things; enter into the joy of your master." Then the one who had received the one talent also came forward, saying, "Master, I knew that you were a harsh man, reaping where you did not sow, and gathering where you did not scatter seed; so I was afraid, and I went and hid your talent in the ground. Here you have what is yours." But his master replied, "You wicked and lazy slave! You knew, did you, that I reap where I did not sow, and gather where I did not scatter? Then you ought to have invested my money with the bankers, and on my return I would have received what was my own with interest. So take the talent from him, and give it to the one with the ten talents. For to all those who have, more will be given, and they will have an abundance; but from those who have nothing, even what they have will be taken away. As for this worthless slave, throw him into the outer darkness, where there will be weeping and gnashing of teeth."

In 27 BC, Augustus Caesar became the ruler of the Roman empire. Petty kings came from near and far to plead for reappointment to their kingdoms. Among them was Herod, king of the Jews. He had to leave his kingdom temporarily in the hands of others while he sought continuance of his rule. Those to whom he entrusted the kingdom were responsible to Herod for how they administered the kingdom in his absence. If they did poorly and he was returned to power, they stood to suffer. If they served him well but Herod was not reinstated, they stood to suffer from Herod's enemies. The best solution was to be absolutely loyal to the side to which they were committed, and at least they would be able to do whatever they did in good conscience.

Jesus told a story that may have been based on just such an event. A man had to go away for a while and he entrusted his goods to his servants. To one he entrusted five talents, to another two talents, and to another one talent. A talent was a measurement of weight and if the item measured were, for example, silver, the value of the talent might be $1,000. That may not sound like an enormous sum to us in our inflationary times, but consider that as recently as 2005 the average worker in India earned 91 cents an hour. One thousand dollars would have been equal to a year of income. Similar conditions existed in Palestine when Jesus told this story. Even the man with one talent would have been considered well-endowed in the estimation of his contemporaries.

Interestingly enough, it is from this very parable that our English word "talent," meaning "a natural gift," has entered the language, and I think it is appropriate for us to read that meaning into this word, as well as other kinds of endowments. Let us consider, then, some of the things this story has to say to us.

The first thing this parable acknowledges is that all humans do not have the same number of gifts. In the parable, one person is given five, another two, and another one talent. And some persons' gifts are intensified because they have received them all in one field. Surely Shakespeare must have received five in literature, Michelangelo five in art, Edison five in inventive ability.

Faced with these kinds of persons who are so richly endowed, the one-talent person is apt to feel "What can I do? I am so poorly endowed I can't make much of a contribution to life." But in fact, every talent is needed in the economy of things. The one-talent person is the foundation upon which most of our social structures are built. We have a piano at home on which there is a particular key that periodically fails to strike. When that happens, my wife asks me to fix it. I point out that she has 87 other keys to choose from. They ought to be enough. But she insists that without that key making its contribution she cannot play what she needs to play. We humans are like the notes on a piano keyboard: If we hold back our contribution because we only have one sound, then we are responsible for an incomplete and unsatisfying performance.

Therefore, instead of being negative about the inequality of our endowments, let us be positive about what we can do with what we have. Remember that favorite children's story "Stone Soup"? Some hungry soldiers came into a town looking for food. Everyone in the town was afraid to share, so they claimed to have no food. The soldiers got a huge kettle, filled it with water, threw a large stone in the pot, built a fire under the kettle, and began to stir. When the curious townspeople asked the soldiers what they were doing, they answered that they were making stone soup. "This soup is delicious," said one soldier, tasting the soup. "What it needs is a little cabbage." One villager said, "Well, I can provide a cabbage," which he did. Item by item the soldiers told the curious villagers what would make the soup better: a few carrots, some celery, turnips, potatoes, onion, salt, parsley. One by one the items were brought forth. Finally the soldiers announced that a piece of meat would make the soup exquisite, and a family brought forth that treasure. Indeed, the soup was exquisite. All had overcome their fear, invested the one thing they had, and there was plenty for all.

Norman Cousins, in his assessment of Albert Schweitzer, said that when Schweitzer decided to go to Lambarene, Africa, he knew well enough that thousands of doctors could not adequately meet the needs of Africa. But the fact that he could not do *everything* never stopped him from doing *something*. No one person could be the total answer, but one person could be part of the answer.

Our gifts differ not only in number, but in kind. One person may be endowed with wealth. Someone told me that anyone can become a millionaire if he keeps clean, rises early, works hard, and has a rich uncle who dies and leaves him a million dollars. The last part is the hardest part. Yet there are those who have become millionaires without it. Regardless of how wealth is acquired, the question addressed by this parable is: "How are you using what you have received?"

Some have the gift of time. In a congregation where I served there were quite a number of retired men. Some of them gathered at the church on Monday mornings and provided services that kept our church in working order. They were not necessarily trained in carpentry or plumbing, but they did things in those areas and saved the church thousands of dollars. Others took training in how to teach people to read. They were not necessarily trained as teachers, but they gave of their time to help others. They told me of the satisfaction they felt when a student of theirs became self-reliant.

The endowments that other people possess are their skills. Two nurses at that church volunteered to establish a parish nurse program in the congregation. Using training they already had, they provided a health ministry to people associated with the congregation.

For still others, the gift may be robustness of body, sharpness of mind, eloquence of speech, or wide-ranging influence. Our gifts are not the same but to focus on the differences may only smother initiative. The final reckoning is not based on how much we started out with, but on what we have done with what we had. Our responsibility is proportionate to our gifts. All of us have received something.

Another thing this parable appears to encourage is risk-taking. The fellow in the story who received one talent to invest hid it, made nothing of it, returned it to his master intact, and was condemned for so doing. That may seem rather harsh to us. After all, he didn't squander the money; he didn't abscond with it; he didn't spend it on himself; he didn't use it to hurt others. He was just being cautious, prudent, and protective. If the truth were known, he was just plain scared. He couldn't cope with the possibility of losing it, so he took no chances and wound up gaining nothing. The implication of this parable is that it is better to try at a venture and fail than to play it safe and show no improvement of the gift one has been given.

Early in his career, Ernest Borgnine was working with Spencer Tracy on a film titled *Bad Day at Black Rock* when he was offered the chance to play the lead in a small black-and-white film written by an unknown television writer named Paddy Chayefsky. Borgnine, frustrated with always being cast to play heavies, told Tracy that he was leaving for New York to do the part. Years later Borgnine recounted on a television talk show that Spencer Tracy thought this would be a big mistake and Borgnine should be content to be making a good living as a character actor. "You're gonna make a little black-and-white film," he lectured Borgnine, "no one's ever gonna hear of it, you're gonna think you're a star, and you're not gonna be a star." "Spence," Borgnine told him, "if I don't try it now, I'll never know." Borgnine went on to make the film *Marty* and was nominated for an Academy Award along with Tracy. As Borgnine went up to collect his Oscar, he passed Spencer Tracy, who said to him: "You never listen, do you?" Perhaps Borgnine did listen, but to a different voice.

The theologian Reinhold Neibuhr tells a parable about Jesus' parable. It is the story of a young man who left his home in Kansas to be a sailor on a tall-masted sailing ship. On the third day out to sea, the new sailor was commanded to take the watch in the crow's nest, high up the mast. After climbing about halfway up the mast he stopped. He was frozen in fear, not able to finish climbing up, and too proud to slink back down and admit in front of the seasoned sailors that he was afraid of heights. So he simply clutched at the mast and did nothing with the responsibility he had been given. In the story Jesus told, the servant who was given the stuff of life and told to invest it, to risk it for the sake of his lord, could not bring himself to do anything. He froze. He only clutched the talent, never giving it or himself a chance.

Jesus' parable gives a further warning that if we fail to use what God has given us, we lose it. The fellow who didn't invest his talent eventually lost it. That is not an arbitrary sentence on the part of an unfeeling judge, it is simply an observation about the law of life: the singer who doesn't use her voice loses it, the trumpeter who doesn't play the trumpet loses his lip. Most of us are probably exposed to a foreign language, but unless we use it, it is probably gone. There was a time when I used to be able to do geometry, but

I haven't thought about geometry for 45 years. Now I would be lost if asked to demonstrate a theorem.

It is the same with regard to career decisions. A member of my family spent most of his life as a house painter, but his favorite thing in the world was to read the business opportunities. He wanted desperately to do something else. But he was afraid. He had a family to support. He had been through the Depression. What if he quit painting and put his meager savings into a business that failed? He always entertained the fantasy and traveled to many places looking at possible ventures, but he never took the chance, and as he got older the likelihood became more remote until the possibility disappeared.

It is the same with our opportunities to show love. In his book *Living, Loving, and Learning*, Leo Buscaglia speaks of one of his students, a girl who shared a poem she had written. She titled it "Things You Didn't Do." She says this:

> Remember the day I borrowed your brand new car and I dented it?
> I thought you'd kill me, but you didn't.
> And remember the time I dragged you to the beach, and you said it would rain, and it did?
> I thought you'd say, "I told you so." But you didn't.
> Do you remember the time I flirted with all the guys to make you jealous, and you were?
> I thought you'd leave me, but you didn't.
> Do you remember the time I spilled strawberry pie all over your car rug?
> I thought you'd hit me, but you didn't.
> And remember the time I forgot to tell you the dance was formal and you showed up in jeans?
> I thought you'd drop me, but you didn't.
> Yes, there were lots of things you didn't do.
> But you put up with me, and you loved me, and you protected me.
> There were lots of things I wanted to make up to you when you returned from Vietnam.
> But you didn't.

If God has situated you in a relationship where you have the opportunity to express love, the opportunity is a gift. Seize the moment. Do it now.

This parable also speaks of accountability. The stewardship of one of the servants was found wanting. There is no way to skip judgment. One way or another, we must turn in a report.

We may think this accounting for how we have used our endowments is something that comes at the end of life, but the accounting process is going on continuously during life. We do not have to wait until the end of life to know how we are doing. We pay our bills monthly. We pay the IRS as we go. We pay the utilities regularly. It's easy to know how we are doing in our responsibilities to those people. All we have to do is to check the statement. That same process can help us know how we stand in regard to the Owner of all things.

Ray Knudsen, an Episcopal priest in San Fernando, overheard his three small boys talking about what they would like to inherit when their father died. The oldest son wanted his dad's watch. The middle one wanted his ring. The youngest son said, "I want all of Dad's checks." The oldest boy responded: "Mark, you wouldn't get a thing! They are worthless. There is nothing of value there." Pastor Knudsen thought perhaps his oldest son had heard the old song:

> There's nothing left for me
> From last month's salary.
> I live in memory
> Among my canceled checks.

But as Pastor Knudsen reflected on that, it occurred to him that perhaps there was something in his checkbook of greater value than his oldest son was aware. "Actually," he thought, "in my canceled checks there is the story of my life — the only autobiography I will ever write: A record of my hopes and dreams; a record of my values and priorities; a record of purchases and expenditures." How about your canceled checks? They are a monthly accounting of your values, priorities, and life. How are you investing those talents God has put at your disposal? (reported in *Pulpit Resource*, Vol. 9, No. 4, p. 24).

While the parable is told in such a way that we focus on the missed opportunity of the one-talent servant, the responsible use of endowments by the other two servants is rewarded. The reward for work well done is more work to do: "You have been trustworthy in a few things, I will put you in charge of many things," says their master (v. 21). The more we exercise a gift or proficiency, the more we are able to tackle. Each of us finds it so in life. The reward for investing our gifts is more to be responsible for, not less. One part of us would like life to become easier, but another part of us responds to the call of new challenges.

Some years ago I called on a lady who attended the church I was then serving, and I invited her to become active in our church. "Oh no," she said, "back in Iowa I did enough for the Methodist church to last two lifetimes. Why, the road to heaven is paved with all those apple pies I baked for church dinners. Now I'm going to rest." Well, I wouldn't for one moment want to detract from yesterday's service, and I don't dispute the need for a change of pace in what we are doing, but if we still have reasonably good health, and if we have been fortunate enough to have rendered service in the past to God or humanity, then our call is to continue and not to stop. That same lady called me subsequently and told me that she wasn't getting as much out of her relationship to our church as she did from her church in Iowa, so she wanted something to do. No more apple pies! But she wanted to be useful. She began calling on shut-ins instead and found it to be rewarding. She was getting back in proportion to what she was putting in.

I close with this. A guest preacher in a rural church arrived at the little church early and went into the narthex, where he noticed a little box affixed to the wall. He thought that it was one of those boxes to receive offerings for the poor, so he put in a dollar. At the close of the service at which he preached, his host took him out to the narthex and explained to him that the church was so small and so poor that they didn't have any money to pay guest preachers, so they put that box on the wall for people to make contributions. As he opened the box he said, "You've done better than most — there's a dollar in it today." That preacher went home and at dinner that day, he told the incident to his family. One of his children said, "Gee, Daddy, if you'd put more in you would have gotten more out."

That is what it comes down to for every one of us. When confronted with our opportunities, if we will put more in, we will get more out.

Christ the King Sunday
(Proper 29 / Pentecost 24 / Ordinary Time 34)
Matthew 25:31-46

Who Cares?

When the Son of Man comes in his glory, and all the angels with him, then he will sit on the throne of his glory. All the nations will be gathered before him, and he will separate people one from another as a shepherd separates the sheep from the goats, and he will put the sheep at his right hand and the goats at the left. Then the king will say to those at his right hand, "Come, you that are blessed by my Father, inherit the kingdom prepared for you from the foundation of the world; for I was hungry and you gave me food, I was thirsty and you gave me something to drink, I was a stranger and you welcomed me, I was naked and you gave me clothing, I was sick and you took care of me, I was in prison and you visited me." Then the righteous will answer him, "Lord, when was it that we saw you hungry and gave you food, or thirsty and gave you something to drink? And when was it that we saw you a stranger and welcomed you, or naked and gave you clothing? And when was it that we saw you sick or in prison and visited you?" And the king will answer them, "Truly I tell you, just as you did it to one of the least of these who are members of my family, you did it to me." Then he will say to those at his left hand, "You that are accursed, depart from me into the eternal fire prepared for the devil and his angels; for I was hungry and you gave me no food, I was thirsty and you gave me nothing to drink, I was a stranger and you did not welcome me, naked and you did not give me clothing, sick and in prison and you did not visit me." Then they also will answer, "Lord, when was it that we saw you hungry or thirsty or a stranger or naked or sick or in prison, and did not take care of you?" Then he will answer them, "Truly I tell you, just as you did not do it to one of the least of these, you did not do it to me. And these will go away into eternal punishment, but the righteous into eternal life."

When Vince Lombardi, the eminently successful professional football coach in the 1960s, was asked how he produced winning teams, he declared that any group of naturally endowed athletes could win more games than they lost if they concentrated on the "little things" of the game — the fundamentals. After a close game won by his Green Bay Packers, Lombardi called a special session for Monday morning because he felt his players were losing sight of the small details that guarantee victory. Appearing before his players, he held a football above his head and announced: "Men, we need to review the basics of the game. This is a football." Max McGee, so the story goes, drawled, "That's a little fast, coach. Go over that again."

In the passage we read from the gospel according to Matthew this morning, Jesus has gathered his team — his disciples — around him for one of the last teaching sessions of his career. Throughout his ministry he attempted to help his followers understand the meaning of the "kingdom of God": what it is, who is in it, what is expected of people who are a part of it. He takes this occasion once again to clarify what it means to be a part of God's kingdom. He returns to fundamentals, and in the process he helps us understand how the game of life is to be played. In order to help you remember the fundamentals of Jesus' message in this passage, I offer them as six *S*s, hoping the alliteration will aid memory.

One of the things he says is that scrutiny is part of the process. There comes a time when our conduct is subjected to judgment. He says that nations and people come before the king and there is a separating of people as a shepherd separates the sheep from the goats. The British poet Studdert-Kennedy said that he once had a dream about this scene. In the dream he saw people coming face-to-face with Jesus, and he heard Jesus ask each of them one question: "Well, what did you make out of what was given to you?" Such a question would be a challenge to any of us.

However, the prospect of having to give an accounting of what we have done with the gifts God has given can have a positive impact on our conduct. One morning in 1888, Alfred Nobel, the inventor of dynamite, the man who spent his lifetime amassing a fortune from the manufacture and sale of weapons of destruction, awoke to read his own obituary. The obituary was a result of a simple journalistic error — Alfred's brother had died, and a French newsman carelessly reported the death of the wrong brother. Any person would be disturbed under those circumstances, but to Alfred Nobel the shock was overwhelming. He saw himself as the world saw him — "The Dynamite King," the great industrialist who made a fortune as a merchant of death and destruction. This, as far as the public was concerned, was the entire purpose of his life. None of his other aspirations — to break down the barriers that separated people and ideas — were recognized or given serious consideration. As he read his obituary with horror, Nobel resolved to make clear to the world the true meaning and purpose of his life. And through the final disposition of his fortune, he established the most valued and prestigious prizes given to those who have done most for the cause of world peace, the arts, and sciences (reported by Robert A. Raines, *Creative Brooding* [New York: Collier Books], p. 111). At some point in our lives, Jesus says, we submit to scrutiny and we have to give an accounting.

Jesus goes on to say that the evaluation process elicits surprise. Those at the king's right hand are told they have rendered service to the king himself. They are surprised and say they were not aware of it. The king says that when they were serving others, they were serving him.

Often we are not aware that an act of caring or compassion has any effect beyond our immediate view. Stephen Lewis, formerly Canada's ambassador to the United Nations, told of visiting Pashawar, the city in Pakistan closest to the

Afghanistan border. There, he and a Canadian External Affairs member — whom he identified only as Barbara — met an Afghan poet. For writing a poem critical of the Afghan government, the poet had spent four years in solitary confinement — one of many prisoners of conscience. Now he was free. "How did you get out?" the Canadians asked him. The poet replied that the Afghan government was besieged by a torrent of letters and postcards on his behalf, organized by Amnesty International groups all over the world. Barbara nodded. "Yes, I know," she said, "before I came out here I was a member of Amnesty Group...." Then suddenly she realized that this man, sitting before her, was one of those for whom she herself had written letters back in Canada. And he realized that he owed his release, freedom, and life to this woman and others like her (reported in *Pulpit Resources*, Vol. 18, No. 4, p. 28). Even though they had not known each other, the actions of one had had a profound impact on the life of the other. One day, we too will be surprised to discover whose life we have impacted.

Note further that the story Jesus is telling is about small things. "I was hungry and you gave me food," the king says to those on his right. For most of us, our opportunity to please God will not be the result of some benevolent act that impacts all of humankind. It will be a small act of caring directed toward an individual. W.W. Lax was a British Methodist minister who told a story from his own experience that underscores this point. He served forty years among the people who lived in the East End of London. Once he was asked to visit an elderly gentleman who lay very ill in a one-room flat. When the preacher called, the man rebuffed him by turning his face to the wall and refusing to speak. While the minister was trying to carry on a conversation, he noticed the poverty of the room, the inadequate heat, and no evidence of food. When he left the house he went to a nearby restaurant and arranged for a lamb chop dinner to be delivered to the little apartment.

He called again in a few days and the crusty patient was a little more receptive. On the way home, the preacher left another order for a lamb chop dinner to be delivered. By the preacher's third visit, a radical change had occurred in the man's attitude. He was congenial and smiled several times. He listened as the minister read the scripture, talked about faith in Christ, and prayed before he left. A meeting took the clergyman out of town for a few days, and when he returned to London, he learned that the old man had died. However, a neighbor reported to the minister that the old man's dying words were these: "Tell Mr. Lax it's all right. Tell him that I love Jesus and that I'm going to God. But be sure to tell him it wasn't his preaching or praying that saved my soul. It was those delicious lamb chops" (told by Donald Shelby, Santa Monica Sermons, *The Church In Overalls*, September 20, 1987). "I was hungry and you gave me food... just as you did it to one of the least of these who are members of my family, you did it to me," says the king (vv. 35, 40). In small things love is revealed.

That love is also revealed in simple things. "I was thirsty," says the king, "and you gave me something to drink" (v. 35). Showing that we care doesn't require an elaborate system of social service. William Barclay, in his book *And Jesus Said* (Philadelphia: The Westminster Press, 1970, p. 107), tells the experience of Mabel Shaw, a missionary to Africa, who told her little Bantu children in Africa about giving a cup of water in the name of the Chief, which is what they called Jesus. They were tremendously interested because in a hot country, a cup of cold water can be beyond price. Not long afterward she was sitting on the veranda. Up the village street came a string of porters, obviously exhausted. They sank down wearily at the side of the road. And then something happened. These men were of another tribe; that could be seen from their clothes and from the way they wore their hair, and there was suspicion and often hostility between tribes. Out from the veranda came a little line of primary-age girls. Each had on her head a water pot. They were obviously a little frightened but just as obviously determined to see this thing through. They went out to the tired porters; they knelt before them and held up their water pots. "We are the Chief's children," they said, "and we offer you a drink." The astonished porters knelt in return, took the water and drank, and the girls ran off. They came running up to Mabel Shaw. "We have given thirsty men water in the name of the Chief," they said. In any ordinary village, had these men asked for a drink, they would have been told, "You are not of our village; get water for yourselves." It was reverence for the Chief that bridged the gulf. It is clear that the simple act of the Bantu children would do more to make Christianity real to those porters than any number of sermons.

Long ago Muhammad said, "What is charity?" And then he answered: "Giving a thirsty person a drink, setting a lost one on the right road, smiling in your brother's face — these things are charity." These are the kinds of things that anyone can do. So often, because we can't do something great, we do nothing at all. But there are kindnesses anyone can do. To do them is to walk the Christian way and in the end to win the approval of the king.

Obviously, this message of Jesus makes much of another "S," serving. "I was sick and you took care of me, I was in prison and you visited me," says the king (v. 36). We are being challenged to do for others what they cannot do for themselves. Noted theologian, author, professor, and speaker Henri J.M. Nouwen made a move from the faculty at Harvard Divinity School to the staff at Daybreak — a residential community for mentally handicapped people. What a dramatic transition this must have been — from working with the world's brightest and best under the spotlight of constant recognition, to laboring almost invisibly with people that the world would sometimes like to forget altogether.

A typical day in the Harvard setting might have included lecturing to packed auditoriums, perhaps an outside speaking engagement, an interview with a magazine editor, and some time at the typewriter working on a magazine article or book manuscript.

At Daybreak, the day began by helping others out of bed, bathing, feeding, and clothing them. Tending to their physical, emotional, and spiritual needs as part of a ministry team filled the day. Nouwen shared what led him to make this change.

> Most of my past life has been built around the idea that my value depends on my accomplishments. I made it through grade school, high school, and university. I earned degrees and awards, and I made my career. Yes, with many others, I fought my way up to the lonely top of a little success, a little popularity, and a little power. But as I sit beside the slow and heavy-breathing Adam (a resident of Daybreak), I start seeing how violent that journey was. So filled with desires to be better than others, so marked by rivalry and competition, so pervaded with compulsions and obsessions, and so spotted with moments of suspicion, jealousy, resentment, and revenge.
> (reported in *Pulpit Resources*, Vol. 18, No. 4, pp. 26-27)

In serving those who cannot help themselves, Nouwen heard the voice of Christ: "Just as you did it to one of the least of these who are members of my family, you did it to me" (v. 40).

The final "S" is sovereignty. It is, after all, the king who says to those at his right: "Come, you that are blessed by my Father, inherit the kingdom prepared for you..." (v. 34).

What Jesus was talking about is the kingdom of God. It sounds as though he is saying "Do these good things and you get in." But that runs counter to so much that Jesus and the New Testament say about God's gracious acceptance of us regardless of our merits.

I think what Jesus is sharing with us is not a formula

for how we save ourselves by our good works, but rather a description of how people who have pledged allegiance to Christ live out that allegiance. Acts of caring and compassion toward the least and loneliest demonstrate that a person is a citizen of the kingdom, even when they don't realize what an impact their actions have. As we are involved in these little acts of kindness, we are helping to make the kingdom of God more visible.

Donald Shelby reminds us (Santa Monica Sermons, *The Church in Overalls*, September 20, 1987, p. 7) that when Ignatius Loyola and his band of nine followers went to petition Pope Paul III in the sixteenth century to form the Society of Jesus, the Pope was unimpressed. Although the men arrived in Rome with glittering degrees, doctors of divinity among them, the Pope was still unimpressed. Then came the winter of 1538, the most desperate in Rome's memory. These ten people took upon themselves the burden of the city's destitute. They put the sick into their own beds, begged straw mattresses and food for the rest, and at times had as many as 300 or 400 crowded into a ramshackle residence, which was all they could afford. So spectacular were their efforts that the Pope could no longer ignore them, and in 1540 he granted them the right to call themselves a genuine religious brotherhood — the Society of Jesus (Jesuits). Their actions indicated whose they were.

Undergoing scrutiny, registering surprise, not overlooking small things, involving ourselves in simple acts, serving "the least of these," acknowledging God's sovereignty — these are ways we come to recognize God's kingdom and give evidence that we are part of it. In time, others will notice that the kingdom has come close to them. They may not know what to call it, but they will know something has happened that makes life better.

I close with this. One of the best letters of reference ever received at the University of Alabama Medical School, according to the director of admissions, came from an old mountaineer. The letter read: "I knowed this kid from the day he was born. He played with my kids, helped me with the chores. I don't know if he has sense enough to make it in medical school, but I do know he'll be the kind of man I'd like to come here to take care of me and my folks" (told by Donald Shelby, Santa Monica Sermons, *Final Evaluation*, November 25, 1990, p. 7).

    Jesus would say "Amen!" to that. "As you did it to one of the least of these… you did it to me" (v. 40).

Thanksgiving Day
Luke 17:11-19

Thanks-Giving Is Good for Everyone

On the way to Jerusalem Jesus was going through the region between Samaria and Galilee. As he entered a village, ten lepers approached him. Keeping their distance, they called out, saying, "Jesus, Master, have mercy on us!" When he saw them, he said to them, "Go and show yourselves to the priests." And as they went, they were made clean. Then one of them, when he saw that he was healed, turned back, praising God with a loud voice. He prostrated himself at Jesus' feet and thanked him. And he was a Samaritan. Then Jesus asked, "Were not ten made clean? But the other nine, where are they? Was none of them found to return and give praise to God except this foreigner?" Then he said to him, "Get up and go on your way; your faith has made you well."

A.J. Cronin tells of a doctor he knew who prescribed in certain cases of neuroses what he called his "thank-you cure." When a patient came to him discouraged, pessimistic, and full of his own woes, but without any symptoms of serious ailment, he would give this advice: "For six weeks I want you to say 'Thank you' whenever anyone does you a favor, and to show you mean it emphasize the words with a smile." "But no one ever does me a favor, doctor," the patient might complain. Whereupon, borrowing from scripture, the wise old doctor would reply: "Seek and you will find." Six weeks later, more often than not, the patient would return with quite a new outlook, freed of a sense of grievance against life, and convinced that people had suddenly become more kind and friendly.

In the scripture we read, Jesus brings about the healing of ten persons suffering from leprosy. Nine continued on their way; only one came back to express his gratitude, and he wasn't even a Jew. He was a Samaritan, a member of a group of people Jews looked down on. Jesus makes the observation, sadly I think, that ten persons were healed, and only one returned to express thanks. There are some lessons to be learned here about thankfulness.

The first thing I want to say is that thankfulness benefits the person who is thankful. It provides a much-needed balance in times of difficulty. I was visiting in the hospital some time ago and I had occasion to call on two ladies who were having a particularly difficult time of it. That one lady was in pain was obvious. She was also terribly depressed: in fact she was in tears most of the time. She referred to herself as a big baby and suggested of her own volition that her depression was the result of her own self-pity. She could not think of anything but her own situation and that made her feel low.

The other lady had been in intensive care and knew all of the discomforts and pain of being plugged into a variety of machines and devices. Nevertheless, her spirits were high. She was thanking God for the close attention and constant care she was receiving. She was aware of what others around her were suffering, and she was thankful that her own difficulties were not worse than they were. She was also thankful for what friends were doing for her family while she was hospitalized.

I don't mean to say that people who are ill need to be Pollyanna or thankful for their infirmity, but even in the midst of pain, there is healing to be found in thanksgiving, for it opens our eyes to blessings we might otherwise overlook. Years ago there was a song we used to sing. It was called "Count Your Blessings" (lyrics by Johnson Oatman Jr.). Perhaps it had neither great music nor great poetry, but it was good, practical theology. It went something like this:

> When upon life's billows, you are tempest tossed,
> When you are discouraged, thinking all is lost,
> Count your many blessings; name them one by one,
> And it will surprise you what the Lord hath done,
> Count your blessings, name them one by one;
> Count your blessings, see what God hath done.

One person, going through dark times herself, decided to follow that advice and came up with the following poem:

> One midnight, deep in starlight still,
> I dreamed that I received this bill:
> 5,000 breathless dawns all new;
> 5,000 flowers fresh with dew;
> 5,000 sunsets wrapped in gold;
> 1,000,000 snowflakes served ice cold;
> 100 music-haunted dreams
> Of moon-drenched roads and hurrying streams,
> Of silent stars and browsing bees;
> One June night in fragrant wood;
> One friend I loved and understood.
> I wondered when I waked that day
> How in the world I could ever pay!
> (Courtland W. Sayers, *How Much Would This Cost?* [quoted in *Lection Aid*, Vol. 3, No. 4], p. 11)

If an attitude of thankfulness helps us in time of need, it helps us in good times too. In one of his books, Fulton Oursler tells of his old Negro nurse, Anna Maria Cecily Sophia Virginia Avalon Thessalonians, who was born a slave on the eastern shore of Maryland and who attended the birth of Oursler's mother and his own birth. She taught him his greatest lesson, the lesson of the thankful heart. "I remember her as she sat at the kitchen table in our house," he wrote, "the hard brown hands folded across her starched wrapper, the glistening black eyes lifted to the whitewashed ceiling, and the husky old whispering voice saying, 'Much obliged, Lord, for my vittles.' " "Anna," he asked, "what's a vittle?"... "It's what I've got to eat and drink that's vittles"... "But you'd get your vittles whether you thanked the Lord or not," he said. "Sure, but it makes everything taste better to be thankful," was her reply. After the meal she thanked the Lord again and then said: "You know, it's a funny thing about being thankful — it's a game an old colored preacher taught me to play. It's looking for things to be thankful for. You don't know how many of them you pass right by unless you go looking for them... Take this morning. I woke up and lay there lazy-like wondering what I got to be thankful for now. And you know what, I can't think of anything to thank him for and then from the kitchen comes the most delicious morning smell that ever tickled my old nose. Coffee! 'Much obliged, Lord, for the coffee... much obliged for the smell of it!' "

There came a time when Oursler went through a very trying and bitter period of discouragement and failure. He said the memory of Anna's spirit of thanksgiving gave him a handle to work with and it literally pulled him up and out and onward. Then he was called to the bedside of a dying Anna, old, crippled, feeble. Standing beside her and noting her hands knitted together in pain, he wondered what she would be thankful for now. "She opened her eyes, smiled, and the last words she spoke were: 'Much obliged, Lord, for such fine friends.' " Among the simple blessings of life we so thoughtlessly take for granted, we too need to say, "Much obliged, Lord, for everything" (shared by Charles M. Crowe, *Sermons for Special Days* [New York: Abingdon Press, 1951], pp. 145-146).

The second thing I learn from this incident is that thankfulness not only affects the outlook of the thankful person, it affects the outlook of others. Jesus was disturbed by the ingratitude of the nine, but gratified by the thankfulness of the one. So far as thanksgiving is concerned, it has been said that the mass of people can be divided into two classes. There are those who take things for granted, and those who take things with gratitude. The attitude we assume affects others. To take benefits from God or from other people without a thought or a word of thanks creates a spirit of ill-will. Winston Churchill told of a man who risked his life to save a drowning child. When he delivered the child to his mother, instead of thanking the man, she merely snapped a question: "Where's Johnny's cap?" You can imagine that that man did not go away feeling appreciated.

Gratitude costs so little and means so much. It does people good to be thanked. It is amazing what we can do for others, as well as for our own souls, if we simply pause and say "thank you." A number of years ago William Stidger, a seminary professor, was confronted with the necessity of preaching a Thanksgiving sermon. It was a difficult time and he was in a difficult place. He felt hard-pressed, looking for something affirmative to say. He began to think of the blessings he had in his life and the things for which he was thankful. He remembered a woman who taught him in school and of whom he had not heard for many years. Although it was years ago, he still remembered that she went out of her way to put a love of verse in him, which had been a source of enjoyment to him for years. So he wrote a letter of thanks to the old lady. The reply he received was in a feeble scrawl and it began, "My dear Willie." He was thrilled about that. Stidger was over fifty at the time, bald, a professor, and he didn't think there was anybody left in the world who would call him "Willie." It made him feel years younger right off:

> My dear Willie, I cannot tell you how much your note meant to me. I am in my eighties, living alone in a small room, cooking my own meals, lonely and, like the last leaf of autumn, lingering behind. You will be interested to know that I taught in

school for fifty years, and yours is the first note of appreciation I ever received. It came on a blue-cold morning and it cheered me as nothing has in many years.

Stidger was not sentimental but he wept over that note.

He then thought of other people who had been kind to him. He remembered one of his old bishops who had been most helpful at the beginning of his ministry. The bishop was in retirement and recently lost his wife. Stidger wrote a belated letter of thanks to the bishop. This was the reply:

> My dear Will, your letter was so beautiful, so real, that as I sat reading it in my study, tears fell from my eyes; tears of gratitude. Then, before I realized what I was doing, I rose from my chair and called her name to show it to her — forgetting for a moment that she was gone. You will never know how much your letter has warmed my spirit. I have been walking about in the glow of it all day long.
> (William Stidger, *More Sermons in Stories* [New York: Abingdon Cokesbury Press, 1954], pp. 117-118)

What more needs to be said on that point? Our thankfulness provides great therapy for ourselves and for others.

The third thing I want to say is that thankfulness also opens our relationship with God. The one leper who returned offered thanks to Jesus and praise to God. Thankfulness is the beginning of the religious life. When a person senses that all of life is a gift, he cannot help but be open to the source of life. There is a little table blessing many people teach their children. Perhaps it is the first prayer the child learns. It goes:

> Thank you for the world so sweet;
> Thank you for the food we eat;
> Thank you for the birds that sing;
> Thank you, God, for everything.

It is a simple prayer, but it is the beginning of a perspective on all of life that will help the child to appreciate the blessings of life that will always surround him.

A young college coed from the flatlands of Kansas arrived for her first semester at her new college in New England. She couldn't get over the beauty of the New England hills ablaze with autumn foliage. Her roommates would find her standing and looking at the hills in rapt awe and saying: "Dear God, it's more than we deserve! It's more than we deserve." Those words, I take it, were sincere expressions of gratitude to God.

In his inspirational book *To Kiss the Joy* (Nashville: Abingdon Press, 1983, p. 145), Robert Raines tells of a surprise he got when he rounded a bend on a mountain road on a trip to the West. He was enthralled to see a deep blue lake with ranges of pyramid pines stretching for miles beyond. He was taken aback with the beauty of the scene. He pulled into a turnout to take it all in. A man pulled his car into the turnout as well, got out of the car, opened the trunk, took out a trumpet, and began to play a heartfelt melody of appreciation to the Creator. He was returning thanks, like a leper who returned and glorified God for his gift!

Grateful recognition of the presence of God will often be the determining factor as to whether one goes on to victorious living or down to defeat following a crisis. There is a great hymn titled "Now Thank We All Our God." It is a hymn of thanksgiving, but it was written by a village pastor after the town where he served was almost destroyed by a plague followed by a famine. In 1647, a plague and famine swept across that town and in one year 8,000 persons perished. It almost destroyed a heroic people but some did survive. Their pastor composed this hymn. At first he started it as a prayer for his own family at mealtime. Since then it has found many uses. It was sung at the dedication of Cologne Cathedral, it is sung in the German churches on New Year's Eve, and it even has a prominent place in the Japanese hymnal. Think of these things in its history as you hear the words:

> Now thank we all our God
> With heart and hands and voices,
> Who wondrous things hath done,
> In whom his world rejoices.
> Who, from our mothers' arms,
> Hath blessed us on our way,
> With countless gifts of love,
> And still is ours today.

There is healing for the soul in a hymn like that. If people can sing that way in faith and reverence and thanksgiving, no tragedy can separate them from God.

Giving thanks is good for us, good for those about us, and good for our relationship with God. There is healing in giving thanks. Thanks-giving is good for everybody.

If You Like This Book...

David G. Rogne has also written *Let Me Tell You: People of Faith Speak to Their Times and Ours* (978-0-7880-1869-5) (printed book $12.95, e-book $10.16); *Telling It Like It Was: Preaching in the First Person* (978-0-7880-1794-0) (printed book $11.95, e-book $10.16); and the Pentecost (First Third) section of *Sermons on the Gospel Readings*, Series I, Cycle B (978-0-7880-1900-5) (printed book $35.95, e-book $30.56).

contact
CSS Publishing Company, Inc.
www.csspub.com
800-241-4056

Prices are subject to change without notice.

www.ingramcontent.com/pod-product-compliance
Lightning Source LLC
Chambersburg PA
CBHW071734040426
42446CB00012B/2360